Unfolding Travels

World Travels on a
Folding Bike

GIANNI FILIPPINI

FIRST PRINTING EDITION, 2019

ISBN 9781702339766

FRONT COVER IMAGE BY GIANNI FILIPPINI

INK DRAWINGS BY GIANNI FILIPPINI

IN GRATITUDE TO SIMON STOTT FOR
CORRECTING THE ORIGINAL MANUSCRIPT

WWW.BROMPTONTRAVELER.COM

Table of Contents

UNFOLDING TRAVELS

1. WAVES AND TREES
2. LAND OF SMILES
3. ROCKIES AND BEARS
4. KASBAH AND TAGINES
5. BACK TO THE COAST

6. MANGOES AND CURRIES
7. CANYONS AND MESAS
8. PEAKS AND LAMAS
9. CHASING COLOURS
10. ON THE SILK ROUTE

Introduction

'Twenty years from now you will be more disappointed by the things that you didn't do than by the ones you did... So throw off the bowlines. Sail away from the safe harbour. Catch the tradewinds in your sails. Explore, Dream, Discover.'

The older I get, the more these few words by Mark Twain ring true. They express why I have an unwavering desire for adventure and travel. As far back as I can remember, I have had the persistent dream to be able to discover some of the most beautiful places on this Earth we inhabit. Nothing unusual I am sure. Who hasn't entertained such thoughts as a child, after all? Maybe growing up in a small town at the foot of a narrow valley in the Italian Alps, made it even more of an urge. I have now learnt to appreciate the beauty of that place, but I used to find it boring, isolated and far too small. With high mountains rising on both sides, the horizons were limited, and as soon as I could walk I remember the desire to discover what lay beyond.

Of course I also wanted to become an astronaut, a rockstar or, at the very least, a world class footballer. These dreams soon petered out for lack of interest in physics and maths, a shortage of the necessary mojo, and a predisposition to sport that if it was a colour was just about beige. The desire to travel remained, but growing up I learnt about life's limitations and even that started to feel more like wishful thinking. In my early teens I took up cycling and for the first time tasted the freedom and sense of achievement that a bicycle can bring. On what were mostly local outings, I gained the confidence and strength to be able to ride longer and further. At least I could reach the

- Bronte and me -

tops of those mountains and see for myself what lay on the other side. I never went that far but those first adventures always brought excitement, and with this, I guess, some seeds were planted.

Years passed and I became aware that to travel money was needed and, when that was available, there was never enough time. Still, I never gave up that dream and sometimes persistence brings about the right twist of fate. Whether I was conscious of this or not, decisions were taken and each time I reached a crossroads it was clear to me which turn I should take. As an adult I found myself blessed with the ability to take at least a couple of extended holidays a year. I was almost ready to throw off the bowlines and set 'sail'. What was still lacking was a little courage that some might call recklessness rather than bravery.

I still had two main questions:

Would it be dangerous?

Probably more than staying at home or spending holidays in an all inclusive resort. In hindsight, far less dangerous than if I was to believe the newspapers or the daily news. We are instantly aware of what is happening around the world and what gets reported is mostly bad news. We convince ourselves that anywhere else but home is unsafe. Ultimately these are just thoughts and they don't reflect reality.
To quote Mark Twain again:

'I have been through some terrible things in my life, some of which actually happened.'

What I have since discovered is that wherever one goes, one mostly finds welcoming and generous people. My wrong perceptions were challenged the most in those places where I was lead to believe I should never go. Invariably they turned out to be some of my most memorable trips and fond memories. All that is needed is to be respectful and to welcome each encounter with a smile and an open mind. Beyond visiting interesting sites or admiring some wonderful nature it is the people you encounter that make these travels memorable. What I also found out is that a bicycle makes you more approachable. A cyclist is unlikely to be perceived as a threat by strangers. On the contrary they will often want to talk to you, find out where you are coming from and how far you are going.

Would it be worth it?

This question was best answered with something I once read and that stuck in my mind:

'If you think adventure is dangerous, try routine; it is lethal.'

We all have our own predispositions, likes and dislikes. but this somehow resounded as quite true. It is good to be able to feel satisfied with life no matter where you are or what you do. Arguably that routine comfort can sometimes prevent you from experiencing something very rewarding and new.

Not unlike a child learning to swim, after some familiarity with safe and shallow water you have to trust and let go of your fears. I pushed my boundaries and before long I was cycling further.

Bicycles are incredibly efficient tools. Scientific studies measuring the efficiency of locomotion for various species on the planet, discovered this too. It was found that the condor uses the least energy to move a kilometre while humans ranked a third down the list. During that study someone next wondered what would be the efficiency of locomotion for a man riding a bicycle instead. Surprisingly a human on a bicycle had no competition and the result was completely off the charts.

Ernest Hemingway once said that it was by riding a bicycle that you best learnt the contours of a country. I certainly agree and there is much more I could say. After years of traveling with a bike I feel as if I don't 'really' know a place until I have cycled it. The freedom it brings, the sense of achievement and intimacy with lands and people I meet, always leaves me wanting more. Totally exposed, soaked in each sight and scent, I am able to cover long distances relying just on the power of my legs.

Thankfully I haven't yet stopped living that boy's dream.

Bronte

- Bronte -

Bike touring, like everything else, comes with its frustrations too. I have always passionately hated the logistical difficulties encountered in transporting the bicycle. Ideally one should set off on a bike from home but time constraints and the desire to visit far away places mean that I have often had to deal with planes or trains. With regular bicycles, it had always been quite a performance, lugging around an unwieldy box and begging for it to be accepted and checked in. The start of such a holiday was anything but stress free. The same was true for the return journey, only compounded by the lack of any excitement for a new adventure about to begin.

I started my search for a possible solution. I needed something easier to carry and I began to wonder whether a folding bike would do. I convinced myself that a bike that can be folded and disguised as regular luggage would be the best answer. I would be able to take it along on more journeys and have the added flexibility to cheat and board a bus or a train should I need to. I was sold to the idea and before I knew it, ready to part with some hard-earned cash.

Bronte came into my life on an early spring day. A small package containing a folded origami made of steel was delivered to my doorstep. Some questions dampened the initial enthusiasm. It looked endearingly cute but very much like a toy. I began to wonder whether such a small-wheeled contraption would be reliable and able to carry me that far. Like the wary swimmer analogy, there was only one way to find out. It involved a little courage and a lot of trust. That is how this book was born, and when the adventures you are about to read, really began.

* * *

WAVES AND TREES

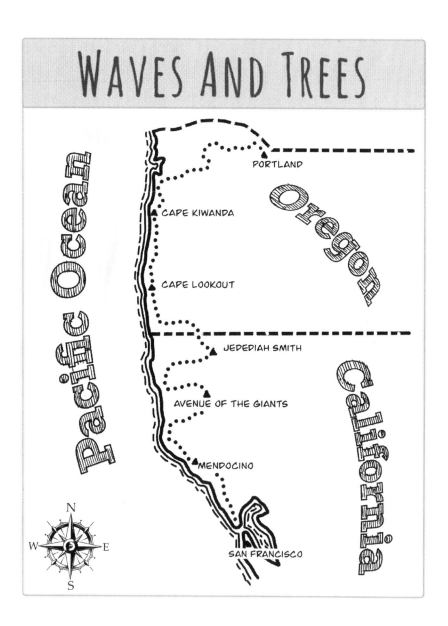

Pacific Ocean

Oregon

California

PORTLAND

CAPE KIWANDA

CAPE LOOKOUT

JEDEDIAH SMITH

AVENUE OF THE GIANTS

MENDOCINO

SAN FRANCISCO

N
W E
S

Waves And Trees

My travel adventures with Bronte were about to begin as I headed with some apprehension to Heathrow airport with an airplane ticket to Seattle. Bronte was brand new and endearingly charming, yet these qualities couldn't prevent me from conjuring up all kind of scenarios; they mostly involved mechanical failures and general doom. Was I just being foolish I thought? Surely the whole thing will collapse under its own weight, leaving me stranded on a road far away from home.

Taking my seat on the packed airplane, I seemed to be the only passenger not employed by Microsoft. I was heading towards uncertainty and discomfort, while the others were travelling to what seemed a much safer corporate event with complimentary cars, buffets and freshly baked croissants. 'Windows' electronic gadgets, a rarity in real life, were popping out from window and aisle seats like mushrooms after a rainy day. I had given my life savings to Apple instead and thought it sensible to keep phone and tablet low profile, out of everybody's sight.

Once at Seattle Tacoma International Airport I found a quiet corner to conceal my well rehearsed routine of unpacking and assembling Bronte back to its original nature. It was a relief to find it exactly as it had been packed, unscathed by any abuse in the cargo. There were no more excuses, the pedalling was about to start.
Seattle was only a brief stopover. I cycled around the centre, catching glimpses of the city that had given us computers, grunge music, online shopping, mugs of coffee and most recently, weed too. Washington State had just legalised the personal use of marijuana, and an

'ecosystem' of little shops and 'cafés' catered for these new needs. Jet-lag was clouding my mind aplenty, all I wanted was a little food and a lot of sleep. The local area turned out to offer nothing better than a baguette at a Subway. I was soon reminded that I had crossed the pond, leaving reticent and prudish England far behind. It was late evening but the middle aged woman in charge of my sandwich was in an excellent mood. She came with parental guidance warnings too. Asking a recommendation on bread types and sizes proved too good an assist for her to resist.

"Small is bad, big is good honey." she remarked.

"You have nice hairy legs. Is your chest hairy too?" she continued, forgetting about my avocado sandwich.

Upon swiping my credit card for payment, she asked to see evidence of my hairy chest. I begged for my credit card not to decline, picked up my sandwich and ran for my life.

I had made a resolution for this trip: traveling alone, I thought there might be times when help would be needed, and I was determined to drop some of my ingrained cynicism and learn to trust strangers a little more. This adventure had hardly started when my good intentions were put to the first test. At Seattle Union Station, I was trying to make sense of a map pointing to the elusive bus stop for the Portland service. After a little toing and froing and a lost look painted all over my face, a young man approached me. He was sporting a large smile promising all the help he could give.

"Are you looking for something?" he asked.

Alarm bells rang; the old habits were back, immediately casting doubt on the shifty nature of the character. I remembered my resolution nonetheless: trust, trust, trust...

I managed a faint, unconvincing yes and added:

"Would you know where the bus stop for Portland is?"

"I am your man, call me Ken." he said. "Aren't you lucky I was passing by."

That remains to be seen, I thought to myself.

"Where are you from?" he asked.

"From Italy."

"Seriously...? You are Italian?" Ken was now beaming with joy.

"What a coincidence. My girlfriend is from Italy. She has just inherited a castle in Aosta."

The unexpected connection made him even more keen to assist.

"I point people to the right bus stops every morning."

"It's part of my Art degree assignment." he stated with confidence.

Maybe the old habits were right after all. What kind of Art degree could possibly involve helping strangers at a busy junction? Social Science, Statistical research, or even Psychology maybe, but Art? I couldn't make any sensible link and after minutes of bonding I was none the clearer about where I should go. Suspicion crept in as I lowered my trust levels by a notch or two.

"By the way, that bus stop you are looking for? I know exactly where it is."
"All I ask for is a ten dollars donation to support my charity..."

Charity? What kind of charity charges such extortionate fees?

To Ken's credit, he did walk me to the right place. I asked for a student discount and got away with a fifty percent reduction. Quite a bargain. He stretched his arm and accepted my five dollars, moaning that it would hardly cover his costs. Relieved, I boarded the bus and was soon fast heading south into Oregon under an angry, cloudy sky.

I was looking forward to Portland. It had a reputation of being the cycling capital of the United States. Cyclists, considered a pest in most American cities, had acquired some status. Drivers, at the wheel of armoured tanks, turned into patient pussycats at the first sight of a bicycle nearing their path. Busy traffic intersections would come to a standstill as soon as any form of human powered vehicle loomed on the horizon. Everyone stopped in reverence, waiting for the object to decide where it wanted to go.

I started the journey under a persistent rain, sealed in my best water repellent gear. The drizzle and foggy views turned my interest to some rather unusual road signs. I discovered that I could 'Adopt a highway'. For those more inclined to gambling, there were wise words pasted on a colourful casino advert: 'Lottery games should not be played for investment purposes'. The soggy start dampened any plans for camping, and once I had reached Forest Grove I ducked for cover into the first motel I could find.

The next day, the road twisted and turned past Gales Creek, following the Wilson river. A day on the bike seems a condensed version of a lifetime. One moment you are restless and bored along plain stretches of road, the next you ache and strain, climbing the steepest hills. You learn to never give up, your tenacity repaid by an effortless freewheel down the other side. You smile again, hardly able to contain your joy. I caught the first glimpses of the sparkling sea, my final destination for that day, my bliss for the next few weeks. I descended the mountain starting to taste the Pacific Ocean on my lips.

- Gales Creek, Oregon, USA -

I arrived in Tillamook, seriously late for lunch. The chatty guy behind the counter at Fat Pizza's was pleased to have an Italian guest, as if he hoped for a seal of approval. After the first ride and the long wait, his pizzas tasted ever so good. Our discussion turned technical, delving into the intricacies of dough, ovens and toppings. I confessed my mistrust of anyone considering blasphemous ingredients such as pineapples, bananas and the like. His facial expression changed. With a hint of sadness he pulled out from the oven his latest work of art. A very blasphemous Hawaiian pizza. He shifted attention to a local competitor who had sold himself to the devil and was now serving pizzas topped with M&M's.

Dusk began to fall on Cape Lookout as cyclists started trickling into the campground. I started making acquaintances from the growing community of pedalling nerds. There was a girl from Portland excited by her first experience cycling and camping on her own. There were three Germans from Munich who had been riding all the way from Calgary, ginger-haired James from California and Kevin, riding for Canada. There was only one road and, unless you were one of those few eccentrics riding North, only one way to go. The wise prefer not to argue with the prevailing southerly winds. Our paths were bound to cross again and again, for many days to come.

My backside, more used to soft cushions and armchairs, was trying to cope with the unforgiving nature of a new bicycle saddle. Brooks leather saddles were a popular choice for long distance travellers. These elegant seats had quite a reputation for needing some time to be broken into. The internet had been full of reviews going into detail about the many aches and pains. Most confirmed that eventually the saddle would give in, taking the shape of your body and providing the ultimate levels of comfort. I still had faith, but it was the most unforgiving piece of leather. I wondered whether it was my body that was taking the shape of the saddle instead.

The first night in the tent was exciting, if not as restful. I woke up in the early hours of the morning hearing a rattling noise and some German cursing. I thought it was some kind of mutiny in the Munich camp. Later I discovered that the real culprit had been a large and determined racoon. It was the talk of the morning. We all heard of its bravery, sliding under the outer tent in order to get hold of a food bag and then refusing to let go despite the constant German hammering with a stick. The day was spent cycling in the company of Kevin and James. We passed through the unusual scenery of Sandlake Road, where clusters of pine trees pierced through sand dunes blown up from the seashore by the strong winds. After almost ten years, I rejoined Highway 1, the road that hugs the Pacific coast from Canada to the Mexican border. It would take me all the way south to San Francisco.

After only two days on the road and a little rain I couldn't resist the temptation of the first laundromat signs. At the campsite, Kevin offered to share some hot rice, vegetables and sausages that tasted ever so good after a day on bananas. I also discovered what the cylinder shaped mystery that stuck out at the rear of his bike was. It was a carefully wrapped traveling guitar whose damp strings by now struggled to keep in tune. If Kevin was a mobile grocery, James was the mobile liquor and pharmacy store. His loaded panniers carried a thorough selection of medicines, whiskies and beers. He carried drugs for obscure ailments and enough alcohol to cheer up even the most despondent cyclist.

My body was getting adjusted to the long rides and felt more comfortable. After Waldport the scenery and the weather improved too. Our progress slowed as we often couldn't help but stop and try to take it all in. The ocean was sparkling in all its glory. A mobile band of American teens carried assorted instruments on their bikes: guitars, harmonicas, a selection of drums, as well as some recreational herbs and booze. More often than not, I found them by the side of the road, trying to fix their rickety bikes. For sure they were having the time of their life. I loved playing my guitar. Before leaving for this trip, the simple thought that I would not be able to see or play one for weeks, set off panic attacks.

That night at Jessie Honeyman hiker biker site there were eight cyclists, three guitars, some beautiful voices and portable drums; I was relieved. After watching the spectacle of a bright red sun disappearing behind the sand dunes before diving into the ocean, we all played and sang together, a rambling orchestra in a cathedral of giant trees.

A few lessons were learnt along the road too. Science didn't always feel right on a bike. Each mile felt way longer than the official 1.6 ratio to a kilometre. Most cyclists riding the Pacific Coast didn't know when they started their journey let alone where they were going to. 'Howdy' was a local greeting and not a recommendation to get off my bike struggles and drive a german car instead. Finally, biscuits and gravy was not a joke but one of Oregon's favourite breakfast perversions.

Several downpours meant that by Coos Bay I was developing an affection for launderettes. I left Green Lightning Laundry quite disappointed. A greedy owner and lack of competition meant that a prepaid card had to be used for pretty much everything but breathing; fares were verging on the extortionate. During the day I kept count of all the food it took to ride my bike. By early afternoon I looked at my list and was horrified; I had munched a packet of nine large chocolate brownies, five bananas, two Seven Eleven cheese and jalapeno taquitos, one litre of almond milk, two slices of chocolate cake and two boiled eggs. If I added the energy drink expenses, my costs were equivalent to running a midsize sports car, without the speed.

For once I treated myself to a motel room. All television channels agreed on one thing, tomorrow would be a glorious day. However, despite the consensus, I began my ride wrapped in a thick blanket of fog. It lasted for the early part of the morning, until the rising sun burnt off the mist, unveiling a memorable landscape. The rest of the day came as advertised; blue skies, ocean vistas to my right and a strong tailwind pushing me on, faster than my legs could ever spin. By lunchtime I had covered two thirds of my planned day. I basked in the sun on a bench outside a café in Langlois, watching the highway life pass by. Later I joined the Mexican Express, two young sisters from Southern California, riding fast racing bikes all the way to the Mexican border. They were fascinated by the looks of Bronte. They insisted on taking some pictures and, I am sure, wondered how much further it would be able to take me.

I was riding along the most spectacular coastline, Highway 1 at its best. I followed its contours up and down a series of high cliffs with breathtaking vistas and the splashing soundtrack of the crashing waves. Humbug Mountain camping site was nestled in a deep narrow valley. I had hardly started pitching my tent when Kevin and his traveling guitar appeared. He had the large and satisfied grin that seemed a constant on any cyclist's face.

- Port Orford, Oregon, USA -

The evening turned chilly so we bought some logs and sat by a warm fire chatting and singing songs with his out of tune strings. We were entering bear territory too; it was about time to gain some Canadian wisdom.

Bears are not an exact science. What was meant to reassure me had far too many variables and I ended up feeling even more scared.

"If you meet a grizzly bear with a cub, play dead." Kevin calmly explained.

"If he is on his own, climb a tree."

Quite straightforward and sensible advice, were it not for the complication that bears come in different shapes and colours and what is a sensible course of action with one, means certain death with another.

It got even worse.

"If you meet a black bear, make yourself look big." he continued.

"If he starts chasing you, always fight back."

Then there were brown bears; a bit of a mixed bag that needed custom made, quick decisions. By the end of the lecture I was knowledgeable and afraid; I tightly zipped my tent ready for a jittery night.

Kevin followed 'Cycling The Pacific Coast', a detailed day by day guidebook for the route from Vancouver Canada to the Mexican border. This cycling bible announced the next day as the most impressive one on the coast. Bathed in sunshine, we were eager yet again to be surprised and awed. The winding road played hide and seek with the ocean, briefly leaving the shore to rejoin it around the next bent, unveiling breathtaking views no words could describe. The ocean unfolded in front of our eyes, scattered with steep rocky islets and crags, waves twinkling and shining in the reflected light.

I had long forgotten my resolution. While climbing a steep hill I heard the kerfuffle of a noisy pickup truck, hooting his loud horn. Immersed in my effort I first thought it might be some kind of road rage or abuse. The truck overtook me, pulled to one side and stopped at a distance, waiting for me. Was I about to be beaten up or robbed? I considered my options, adrenaline running wild. As I reached the vehicle, the kindest of souls pulled down his window and with a beaming smile handed over my sunglasses. He had found them at the restaurant and thinking they must be mine, had set off quite a distance in order to return them. I laughed, thanked him gratefully and remembered once more that I should trust. We reached Brookings Harris Beach on Canada's Thanksgiving day. A few of my fellow travellers being Canadians, there were frantic preparations to throw an improvised party with a bonfire and lots of food and beer.

I had run out of Oregon and welcomed California. After crossing the State border I spotted a signpost pointing to Jedediah Smith State Park. I had read the campsite within the Park had some of the largest redwood groves in the world. It was a stone's throw from where I was but in a different direction than I had planned; I couldn't resist the temptation and decided to veer inland, away from the coast. Arriving in the early afternoon I had plenty of time to explore the bewildering trees, some of them higher than a hundred metres and over two thousand years old.

The hiker biker site, a little removed from the main part of the campsite, was located in the best spot, right by the river. Having temporarily left the cycling caravan, this meant that for the first time I would be alone for the night. Spread around the extensive campsite grounds there must have been only a dozen guests or so. There were no signs of other cyclists at the hiker biker site. I could take my pick and choose the best spot, my tent pitched right under four enormous redwood trees like sentinels standing guard.

An eerie feeling of isolation amplified the distressing warnings I had read on the signboards by the entrance gate. They informed and scared visitors, claiming that bears, as well as mountain lions, had been recently spotted in the area. The dimming daylight and the long shadows of the thick forest played with my nerves, turning every faint sound into a life threatening sign. I recalled the Canadian lecture; I painted gruesome pictures of wild animals in my brain and pondered the doomed fate of a stranded biker seeking cover behind the flimsy walls of his tent. It got dark and I felt very small among those groves; weary of too much silence I resorted to my portable radio, turning it on full blast. Every allotment featured a sizeable, bear-proof metal box meant as storage for all food and scented things. I pondered locking myself into one for safety, leaving all the food in the tent instead.

Luckily I woke up the following morning, still intact and unchewed.

Highway 99 climbed its way through striking redwood groves. Struggling up the hill, I heard my name being called; it was Andrew and Suzanne, the Canadian couple I had met a few days earlier. They had also stayed at the camp but had arrived much later and decided to not use the hiker biker site, opting to pitch their tent next to the camper vans instead. During the day I often crossed paths with an Alaskan girl traveling by car. She was not much faster than I was. Yes, nature here was conducive to lots of pauses for contemplation but to my shock and horror, I discovered her slow progress was due to the fact that she often stopped for quick dips in the ocean. She told me how she found the October ocean temperatures rather inviting. Crossing through Klamath, I entered Yurok territory, a Native American reserve where I could witness for myself the upsetting outcome of past colonisations. People who had once thrived and communed with the bounties of Mother Earth had been left landless. A lot of them seemed resigned to spending the rest of their lives sitting in front of slot machines, hypnotised by the flashing lights. I felt sad. They seemed the most friendly and dignified of people, with a gentle smile and an old wisdom imprinted in the wrinkles of their sunburnt faces.

Paying for some groceries in Klamath Market, I was told that the largest tree in the world had recently been discovered not far from here. Luckily its whereabouts was kept secret to preserve the surrounding groves from succumbing to mass tourism and inevitable ruin. Newton Drury Scenic Parkway was to be my next treat. After the initial harsh climb up the hill I was rewarded with a long and twisty descent through a forest of the largest trees I had ever seen.

John Steinbeck expressed best what I felt in front of such majesty:

'The redwoods once seen, leave a mark or create a vision that stays with you always...from them comes silence and awe. The most irreverent of men, in the presence of redwoods, goes under a spell of wonder and respect.'

Arriving at Elk Prairie Creek, I recognised James's face, standing proud by his trusted bike. It wasn't too long before the Canadian contingent arrived too. The air at dusk was getting fresh and the light grew dim when we heard some clattering noise, announcing Jack's arrival. His bike travelling was not for leisure like most of us; for him it was the cheapest way to get to some seasonal work instead. Coming all the way from Montana, a banjo strapped around his neck, he had decided that he might as well take the long route and enjoy the scenery along the way. A little sidetracked, he was by now wondering if he would ever make it on time. He was surviving on a diet of peanut butter and jam sandwiches, purchased with government food stamps; his long commute was for a job on a farm in Redway, 'weeding grass'. Of course, he was eager to point out, for medical purposes only. Jack was full of good stories typical of someone thrown into an adventure in which he never intended to take part. What he most wanted to know was whether we had also met any new born Christians on the road. He had met plenty, to the point of becoming almost scared. He wondered whether they were messengers sent to correct his wayward ways and his lack of faith.

"They all try to stop me and tell me how Jesus has changed their lives." he said.

"Has anyone crossed the mad woman today?" he asked.

"I was riding at full speed yet she chased me on foot yelling that she will take her backpack all the way to Jerusalem."

He was born in a city whose economy had recently been boosted through accepting mountains of trash from New York City. Talking rubbish, he went on to tell us about his future dream. Full of excitement he told us that there were large cargo boats ferrying trash from Hawaii to San Francisco. They made the reverse journey all empty, and his best hope was one day to hop on one, getting a free ride to paradise.

Best signpost award for the day:

'Having a two years old is like using a blender without a lid'

It was a freezing morning, the campsite immersed in a thick, chilly mist clinging to my tent. Jack, very late for work, was the first to leave, disappearing in the morning fog, his banjo strapped around his shoulders and a fear of God following. For days I had tried to put it off, but James was determined to finally introduce me to 'biscuits and gravy'. By now I was generally tired of biscuits but pouring a meat gravy on them sounded uncivilised and mean. For once in my life, I was not looking forward to breakfast. The gravy mess James had been talking about for days was not worth the hype. His bike developed some technical problem too and he had to resort to a hitch hike to the nearest town to get it fixed. I left on my own.

I reached Arcata, with its chilled out vibes of any surfing seaside town. I was looking forward to my stay, were it not for the fact that the hostel I had considered spending the night in, only existed in the fiction of my outdated map. Searching for a good lunch down the high street I saw James, his hands waving at me, waiting in front of the bike store. A magnetic pull seemed to bond us all on these roads, we often parted but were never too far away. It was time for farewells. The joys of riding and sharing this journey with other cyclists came at the expense of slow progress. I was stopping not only when I wanted to but also when others did. I had to stick to my plan and get to San Francisco in time for my return flight. Regrettably I couldn't linger and had to keep pedalling faster and for longer days than I would have wanted to.

There was much anticipation as I approached the Avenue of the Giants, a world renowned stretch of road swerving through redwood groves. I had long wished to be able to cycle it. By ten in the morning I had reached Scotia where the diversion leaves the main highway. I met a fellow Italian cyclist called Valerio, a very active sixty year old man who had traveled the world extensively on his bike.

-Avenue of the Giants, California, USA -

He had lots of stories to share. He had been to some of the most remote parts of the world, crossed Amazonia, Alaska, most South American countries and China, all on his trusted old bike. He told me how, many years before, he had been inspired by a chance encounter with a Spaniard called Pedro. He referred to him as his 'bicycle master'. Pedro's cycling tales of course were epic, reminiscent of old explorers and pioneers. He had cycled through the Iranian revolution completely unaware. He was once caught up in the middle of fighting gangs in Nicaragua, who stopped him and started playing a shooting game, him being the target; real bullets started landing to his left and to his right before the pranksters decided to let him continue his wanderings in peace. I was almost reduced to tears of awe amongst the power of those trees. Valerio told me that in all his travels, he had never seen such beauty.

I met him once more, just before exiting the road in Phillipsville. He was walking by the side of the road, surprised that it had taken twenty-one years for one of his spokes to finally give. Another cyclist was now on the lookout for a hitchhike to get it fixed. I kept quiet but started wondering whether I had some kind of negative mojo causing people's bikes to break down. After a soothing time cycling through the best of the natural world, Garberville was a complete shock. The place seemed to be stuck in the sixties and was a blend of vagrants, hippies and eccentrics, parading mighty hangovers and flowery outfits up and down Main Street. Ahead was the infamous climb up Leggett. I took a right turn onto highway 1, crossed the little bridge and was at the foot of the mountain range that would have brought me back to the ocean. The climb did not merit the gruesome accounts of cyclists drawing their last breaths while attempting the steep gradients. It was a twisting and engaging road instead, culminating in a memorable descent. Heading down the other side, there was a sudden weather change. From the hot sweltering day I dived into a freezing fog that threw me straight into winter.

In these misty conditions I met Max, an Austrian cyclist. Judging from the load he was carrying, he had decided to relocate to California, on a bike. The heavy clutter was piled up high on his trailer and was held together by an inflatable canoe, squashed right on top. He had pushed this trailing nightmare around the US for five months already, and by now sported a long wiry beard as proof. He admitted that the canoe idea had been a little rushed as he had hardly been able to use it. The ups and downs along this stretch of road were breaking his rhythm and playing havoc with his knees; he cycled in bursts. Swaying left and right, he crawled up steep hills to then shoot down on the other side like a bullet, pushed fast by the sheer weight of his moving ordeal.

Lucy's, in Fort Bragg, won hands down the award for best launderette so far. I spent a blissful hour in the morning, simply drying up my soul and my clothes, dampened by the ever present fog of the last few days. Lucy's touched all the soft spots; free coffee, a friendly attendant and a large poster stuck on the wall: 'Keep calm, we have wifi'. I exited this tumble dryers delight and began cycling as a grey soup still lingered in the air, wrapping me tight;

I was getting frustrated with passing by lots of panoramic points that I couldn't see. The fog was so thick that I could hardly make out the faint shape of my wheel, spinning fast right in front of me. A rather shy sun finally pierced the sky in Elk. I stopped and spread open my damp tent on a wooden table, convinced it would soon dry. Of course it didn't. I had a live encounter with a Tourette syndrome case in the shape of a suave looking elderly man. He was appropriately standing right in front of the village church door. He asked where I had come from. I told him I had come from Portland on a bike. 'Jesus Christ...' he started; it was all downhill from there, the men was on a mission, grew in confidence and every other word he used had God portrayed in the most unfavourable ways. Profanities kept falling in buckets, finding a suitable place in every sentence. That evening, I was the first to cross the line at Manchester Bay. Max eventually emerged from the fog with his fully furnished trailer. I was cold and put all my hopes in an aptly named 'bomb burrito', before wearing everything I carried and diving into my sleeping bag.

The following day started nervously, and it wasn't just the fault of a burrito that seemed to have imploded in my stomach. What mostly tested my patience were the gloomy reports on the radio. For several days the forecasts had started with balmy temperatures and promises of scorching sun, before a short disclaimer warning that the coast might experience 'some foggy patches'. I could swear that what I had been cycling through in the last two days were no weeny patches. Today the weatherman was chirpy, announcing blue skies and recommending a generous use of sun creams, sunglasses and wide-breamed hats. Things looked much more sombre from the inside of my tent but I wanted so much to believe him. I unzipped the door of my tent, stuck my head out and lo and behold lost visibility of my stretched hand. More dreaded fog. It began drizzling too. I needed a new plan, or else would risk slogging through another wet day with no chance of seeing anything around me. I was wary of straying from the coast and my careful plans, but more adventures loomed ahead according to the excitement of a local lady I had the bad luck to encounter in Manchester.

On my maps I had spotted a road that turned left up the mountains, highway 253 heading to Booneville. Asking her advice she was all for it and seemed very enthusiastic; her words suggested a wonderful Shangri-la of forests, green pastures and wineries. She closed her sale pitch with the promise that having crossed the mountains the sun would sure be shining and hot.

"Why would anyone stay in this fog!" she enthused.

I couldn't agree more, the last bit touching a nerve or two...

"Was the road steep?" I asked.

"Well, up and down you know..." she said raising her shoulders.

"You will have a great time!"

Admittedly she got quite a few things right: the sun, the cows, the pastoral nature of the surroundings and the vineyards were all there to be admired. A few miles up the mountain I emerged from the darkest fog and was basking in a beautiful and warm morning sun. The rest was not as accurate. After a start with gentle grades the road turned narrow and steep and I began an exhausting roller coaster which consisted of long walks up a mountain followed by quick descents that in a matter of minutes brought me back down to where I had started, ready for the next climb. Our Lady of Manchester's reputation took quite a dive as I panted and cursed my way up and down. I promised myself never again to heed any advice given by sophisticated looking ladies driving Mercedes convertibles down the highway. I persevered and made it to a charming town called Cloverdale: a total wreck, I knew I deserved a motel for the night.

I was nowhere near where I should have been, but often changes bring unexpected surprises. I had a chance 'encounter' with Francis Ford Coppola and took part in a police car chase down the highway. It was early morning when, refreshed and energised by a substantial dinner and breakfast and a decent bed, I was pushed to blistering speeds by a strong tail wind and the fast traffic. The emergency lane was wide and the morning fresh and sunny. A few spots of low fog had nothing to do with the ghastly milky soup I had so got used to. This was rather scenic and if anything, added atmosphere to the hilly landscape scattered with well tended vineyards.

Passing by an impressive farm, I spotted the large golden plated name Coppola, shining above the entrance gate; looking closer I realised it was indeed Francis Ford Coppola who, I had recently read, had developed a great passion for wine. A nasty nail, right outside his gates, found its way up my rear wheel tyre producing a fast and sudden deflating sound... Hollywood glamour gave way to a tyre repair by the side of the road.

I was back on the busy highway; fast flowing San Francisco bound traffic pushed me on at fast speed. I heard the sound of blasting sirens getting nearer and nearer. Blue and red flashing lights appeared as the police car coasted along my side, slowing down three busy lanes of traffic behind it; the loud speaker on its roof announced to all commuters that I should pull to the side and surrender. The oblivious cars didn't seem to mind my little bike rolling down an emergency lane but these policemen were taking their morning patrol seriously. The large officer exited his flashing tank, pistol and handcuffs dangling by his side.

"How long have you been riding on the highway?" he asked.
In these situation I always think it is best to play dumb and exaggerate one's insanity.

- Highway Patrol, California, USA -

"I started in Portland Oregon." I said.

"Do you know that what you are doing is illegal and dangerous?" he asked.

"No. I am so sorry officer... Is it?" It was.

In the end the questioning and the sirens kerfuffle turned out to be only for the best of reasons. The stern looking officer turned into a fatherly figure and said he would escort me off the highway and back to the safety of a quiet road. Flashing lights and sirens went back on as Bronte and I were triumphantly paraded by a police car, around junctions and over bridges, past the enraged stares of the inconvenienced drivers. The law enforcing angel seemed happy that I was heading in the right direction; he wished me good luck but didn't lose sight of me for a good while, in case I was tempted to get back on the highway again.

In less than three hours I had covered sixty kilometres and in Penngrove I satisfied a large appetite with the best, heart attack-inducing burger I could ever wish for. I reached Petaluma and was trying to figure out how to best get to Point Reyes, back on the coast. The local Tourist Information office was empty and quiet, with the melancholy of an end of season resort in the air. The two ladies behind the counter were overjoyed by the opportunity to finally break their boredom and chat to someone. It ended up being much less about Point Reyes than about one of them going to Italy soon and needing directions and recommendations along the Amalfi coast. Realising I had cycled down the Pacific Coast they came around from their desk eager to check the muscles on my legs; Subway flashbacks warned me it was again time to say goodbye.

I followed a most uninspiring D Street that turned out instead to be a surprising discovery; it went through prairies, a reservoir and along the way I could also visit the famous Cheese Factory that had been recommended to me. I reached Point Reyes and was back on the Pacific Coast in time for yet another stunning sunset.

Near Stinson Beach, it got too dark to continue and it was time to pitch my tent on a grassy patch by the ocean where at night curious deer checked who their night's guest could be. The excitement at having almost reached the final destination was bittersweet, mixed with the sad realisation that the joys each day had brought were about to end. Part of me wanted to continue, wishing that time was not a constraint anymore. The best I could do was to slowly take in the last few sights, savouring mile by mile the remaining road to San Francisco. I didn't want to arrive yet. Getting lost trying to find the coastal trail I had walked many years back, seemed an excuse. Sausalito was all the way down behind the mountain, and the grand entrance of the Golden Gate bridge was hiding around few more hills. I climbed up the Headlands in search of a night spot with a priceless view over the bridge.

Forget the Fairmont, at Kirby's Cove spot 1, I had the best view money could have bought. Right in front of my tent door stood the bright red Golden Gate frame reflecting the last rays of a bright red setting sun.

- San Francisco, California, USA -

* * *

LAND OF SMILES

Land Of Smiles

A hot winter break, temples and stupas, spicy curries and smooth roads; I was looking forward to touring Sri Lanka. A few months later and here I was, collecting Bronte from the spinning luggage belt of Bandaranaike International Airport. I unwrapped it like a delicate gift, under the watchful eye of military officers. Bolts, tools and assorted bundles piled up around me, raising their suspicion. One of them didn't like all that clutter and told me I couldn't assemble my bike inside an airport. Still with pieces and parts scattered all over I pleaded for mercy and asked for a little more time.

I began this new journey on a sweltering day. What a great contrast to the cold and grey winter I had left behind. I took the first few timid pedal strokes acquainting myself with the unfamiliar smells, sights and sounds. Ways to and from any major airport in the world are often not the best of places for riding a bicycle. Traffic was not too heavy, rather what I had to learn was a set of unwritten rules. Life on the road followed a strict pecking order. Large trucks were king, followed by buses, cars, then tuk tuk tricycles, often used as taxis, and finally motorbikes. A foreigner on a bicycle ranked nowhere.

I followed the example of local cyclists, determined to not give in to the bullying and earning my space on the lanes. Negombo Beach proved hard to find. The light of day waning, I veered off the main road into a maze of little roads bordered by ads promising incredible sea views and not yet built resorts. Asking for directions didn't help. Whether it was the language barrier or not, nobody seemed to exactly know where they were. Local policemen were no exception, which goes some way towards explaining the pervading traffic mess. Pointing at town names and providing GPS data over enlarged satellite maps, was not much help. Policemen responded with a shrug of the shoulders and a total refusal to admit that we were all standing exactly where we were. I made my first acquaintance with the large population of stray dogs too. They were thin and looking far too exhausted to take an interest in my spinning calves, yet I was undoubtedly drawing more of their attention. While they let a local peacefully cycle past them inches from their noses, my approach always produced some kerfuffle. Lost, I settled for the first bed and breakfast I could find.

Not knowing exactly where I was didn't matter that much. All I had to do was follow the coast, heading north and eventually, despite local's refusals to accept any evidence, I would reach the town of Puttalam. Cockerels in Sri Lanka were perky by four in the morning. They were kind to me too because in such heat, early mornings were the best time for cycling. I was pleased to discover that carrying bottled water was not necessary. Scattered along the road were coconut vendors that for small change skilfully sliced open fresh coconuts. I could then drink the refreshing water and use the sliced top of the shell to scoop the white flesh inside. Unaware of market prices and not yet familiar with the local currency, I was at the mercy of skilled tradesmen. They were asking obscene amounts of Rupees for fruits literally falling off the trees. Prices seemed to decrease the further I moved away from the tourist catch of Negombo Beach. After ten coconuts I had gained the bargaining skills of a prudent Sinhalese housewife and was paying reasonable fees.

"How much is a coconut?"

"Very nice coconut, 90 rupees only for you." was the bait.

"90 rupees? Are you kidding? I just bought one down the road for 50 rupees." I would reply with the authority of experience.

"Ok... 60 rupees...just for you."

The next seller of course wasn't as lucky. I began to enjoy the bargaining banter and took it as a challenge to see how low it could possibly go. It seemed fair to stop when my offer was faced by a stern look and a complete refusal to produce the goods. After a day or so I discovered the real price of a Sri Lankan coconut.

I hadn't done much research on local food before my departure. Everything was mysterious and enticing and often surprised me with unexpected tastes. On one of my first stops I gambled on an interesting looking fish pastry. A few bites into the fried golden ball unleashed a fierce heat and spice overload. I cycled the rest of the day under the syncopated rhythm of unstoppable burps. I had almost reached Puttalam when I met Brian, a British man who had recently set off on a several months bike tour in Sri Lanka and India. We had hardly cycled together thirty minutes when, in a not particularly attractive spot, he announced the intention to stop for a cup of tea. At first I thought he meant buying one from a nearby stall; Sri Lankan tea is of excellent quality, extremely cheap and the pride of the country. Brian had different ideas. In sweltering heat, he produced his camping stove and boiled a mug of water, brewing his trusted sachets of Ceylon tea brought all the way from England. It was four o'clock after all and, even seated cross-legged by the side of a dusty road, he was being a true gentlemen.

After Puttalam I veered inland, away from the ocean, two more days on the plains before starting a slow ascent up mountains of two thousand metres. If it hadn't been for the cheap coconuts and the wonderful people I met, they would have just been a few unremarkable cycling days in the tropics. Endless stretches of road where I kept pedalling towards an hazy horizon with nothing for the eyes to get hold of or look forward to. The strong headwinds and long alternating uphills and downhills in a humid heat, made the cycling harder than planned. I often took rests at the stalls by the roadside. More often than not I ended up meeting the whole family. We sat together and laughed over answers they could not make sense of to questions I couldn't understand. Their curiosity focused on three main topics.

"Where are you from?"

"Italy but I live in England."

Their eyes inevitably lit up with excitement. They were very fond of my answer. England, having had a profound influence on the island since colonial times, was still viewed as a positive example of civilised living and good manners. Italy, as I later learnt, was the most popular destination for locals willing to emigrate for a few years and make some savings.

Next came "Where are your wife and children?"

"Not married and don't have any…"

"But why?" they would ask incredulous.

Whatever I said always failed to convey the sense of a life where I was satisfied to be on my own. Their initial excitement dimmed, hints of melancholy were now painted on their faces; they felt sincerely sorry for my plight.

The third and final thing beyond their comprehension…

"Why are you traveling on a bicycle?"

"I love cycling."

This was the last straw. At that point they would give up on me.

- Anuradhapura, SRI LANKA -

"Why? It is tiring. It's so much easier to take a bus."

This was asked with the kind of sorrowful admiration bestowed on a Yogi devoting his life to penance. Again all explanations were in vain.

It was a young country and I was struck to see so many children everywhere. Clad in impeccably white school uniforms, they would burst into a chorus of greetings or test newly learnt English phrases as soon as they spotted me passing along the road. My replies were always repaid with large smiles, joy painted all over their faces.

I reached Anuradhapura, hanging on to dear life while cycling through the city centre traffic in what seemed like hell on a particularly bad day. One of the ancient capitals of Sri Lanka, it was famous for its well-preserved ancient ruins and sacred Buddhist sites.

It claimed to be one of the oldest continuously inhabited cities in the world and was one of the eight World Heritage Sites in the whole country.

My luxurious abode for the night was managed by Upali, who welcomed me with a northern Italian accent. He had spent almost twenty years working in Italy and had recently been able to return and build an elegant property in style. He introduced me to Vippalu, one of his trusted drivers, who whizzed me around the main sightseeing spots on board his decorated tuk tuk.

I had underestimated Sinhalese dogs. While it was fair to say that they spent most of their days limping in search of shadows, they certainly showed umphhh in the early hours of the morning. Well rested and fresh, they could give a rather convincing chase, testing my stamina and sprinting speed. I had a lucky escape when four enraged dogs set chase. As the rattle and loud barks increased in volume right behind my back, I dug deep for some adrenaline in order to outpace them. They didn't seem mean or determined to give me rabies, I was just being playfully tested. The first mountains appeared in the distance, the landscape turning lush green. Straight roads turned crooked and took on attitude, navigating around rice fields and thick coconut groves.

I saw my first majestic elephant and a monitor lizard too. The latter, luckily not on the road but rather resting still, was half immersed in the cool temperatures of a shallow water ditch. These lizards looked scary, and before my departure I had done a little research   just in case. Encyclopaedia Britannica claimed that while most were harmless to humans, there were certain types that could kill, maim, make ill, or inflict considerable levels of pain. Venomous, very large and quite aggressive, the Sri Lankan Water Monitor was top of the list. They were not endearing animals and should be left alone at all costs.

More gruesome facts followed:

> *'Water monitors are carnivorous. These lizards do not*
> *surprise their prey; they actively pursue them by swimming,*
> *climbing, or running after them. They eat corpses of human*
> *beings, which they have been known to excavate and devour.*
> *Humans bitten by monitors may be injected with venom,*
> *which exposes them to infectious bacteria. This monitor can*
> *also use its whip-like tail and sharp claws as weapons.*
> *Although some reports of people dying from attacks by large*
> *individuals exist, they are probably untrue...'*

Probably?!

> *'Water monitors have been observed eating catfish in a*
> *fashion similar to a mammalian carnivore, tearing off chunks*
> *of meat with their sharp teeth while holding it with their front*
> *legs and then separating different parts of the fish for*
> *sequential consumption...'*

I had read enough to know I should be careful.

I reached Sigiriya with plenty of stops, dispensing greetings to children as if they were candies. I walked up Lion Rock, a World Heritage sacred site. After 1400 steps up the dramatic rock face I reached the top as the sinking sun cast long shadows on tropical green planes down below.

I often looked at tourists getting off air conditioned cars to briefly stop at a roadside stall, their guides busy telling them names of exotic fruits for sale. It always reminded me how lucky I was. I would never have traded the chance to spend long hours each day sweating, enwrapped by the forest, immersed in sounds I had never heard and scents I had never smelt. Able anytime to stop by the side of the road, I

- Sigiriya, SRI LANKA -

could taste sweet fruits whose names I didn't even know. And the smiles of all those children...priceless.

Life at fifteen miles an hour felt just about right. It was slow enough should I want to stop and fast enough when I didn't want to linger. The bike was also wonderful in limiting all touting. Bronte always offered the perfect excuse to say no and to be quickly let off the hook with a smile.

"Here is a beautiful hand woven carpet. What about this wooded carved Buddha? Very good price for you."

"Sorry I can't take them. I am on my bike..."

Precious stones and jewellery were light and easy to carry. I needed a different approach.

"I'm on a bike. I only wish I had any money left to buy diamonds?"

"Taxi for you, I can take you wherever you want and back...."

That one was easy.

When everything else failed, I pretended to have run out of money, forced to cycle instead. It always worked a treat.

Dogs were less bad-tempered than they had been before. A single, half-hearted chase was the perfect time to put into practice some newly learnt skills I had seen being used effectively by an old man at a temple. It involved a little leap of faith. No more pedalling like a maniac trying to outpace them; the trick was to slow down instead, looking straight into their eyes while shouting a 'shooosh' sound and pointing a finger at them. To my wonder, the beasts were tamed, lost any interest and turned into the gentlest of poodles.

Horizons changed from flat forested plains to a view of rising mountain ranges that I would soon climb. I had to reach the old capital, Kandy. These long, steep and winding roads turned out to be much harder due to the extreme humidity and heat. Coconut vendors and trees had disappeared; after hours of slow progress I was running out of water and on the verge of a heatstroke. Spotting a little run down shop, convinced I could finally quench my thirst, I realised that there was no electricity, let alone fridges, in sight. All they were selling were bread and salty snacks, and all the things whose simple sight made me sweat further. Filled with sorrow, I plonked myself on a chair in the shadow of a little patio. The two ladies behind the counter stared at me, wondering what on earth I might have been looking for. The mystery of a foreign cyclist sweating and panting rather than paying a five dollar tuk tuk fare and getting to Kandy like everybody else did! I tried to convey the importance of selling bottled water or any liquid on this hot forlorn mountain road. They only spoke Sinhalese, I probably failed.

Once I reached Kandy I was in for another surprise. I had reserved what, in pictures, seemed a comfortable room at a hotel promisingly named Stone House Suites. After cycling in circles through a maze of narrow lanes winding up and down a hill, the hotel was nowhere to be found. I gave up searching and decided it would be best to seek some local expertise. I folded my bike and waved down a tuk tuk rider, showing him the hotel address, curious to know if he would be able to find it. After a long vain search, we moved a little further up the hill and finally found a Stone House hotel.

By now pretty exhausted, I stumbled through the door, folded bike in one hand with the rest of my gear hanging all over my neck and arms. Two smiling porters, wearing the most elegant uniforms, welcomed me, and in no time stripped off all the weight I was carrying. They lead me through an elegant corridor bordered by fountains and waterfalls until we reached a patio;

"Please sit down sir."

Still in a sweat and in my cycling clothes I was almost embarrassed to take a seat on the luxurious white sofa.

"Can we offer you a cocktail?"

What a contrast with a few hours before, when I would have given a kidney for a drop of water. The porter soon reappeared with a colourful cocktail presented in an elegant crystal flute and a selection of nuts.

"Enjoy sir. Could I have your name sir?"

I gave my name showing my reservation. I felt a little spoilt. The bright lounge room overlooked a tidy lawn with a swimming pool and, being on top of the hill, allowed grand views of the city down below. For the price I had paid it all seemed an incredible bargain. Sipping my complimentary drink I was asked to register. I confirmed I had prepaid for the room and was whisked, bike and all, to the most tastefully furnished hotel room I had ever seen. Beautiful pieces of wooden carved furniture, elegant curtains and drapes, a super king size bed with heeps of cushions wrapped in soft silk, and a fluffy carpet that half buried my feet as I walked. I was shown the large two rooms bathroom, where rows of towels of all shapes and sizes had been arranged and all kind of amenities were on display.

"Do you like the room sir?"

I disguised a faint approval while in the back of my mind I was feeling ecstatic, congratulating myself on what seemed the bargain of the century.

"Thank you sir. Is there anything else I can do for you sir?"
"Enjoy your stay sir."

I dashed to the shower room, rinsing off my daily tribulations as well as hand washing my cycling clothes. Laundry was hanging all over to dry and gave the once tidy bathroom, hints of a narrow street in Naples. Fifty dollars a night had never stretched this far. I sank into the soft bed and just as I was planning to depart for some sightseeing, I received a phone call from the front desk. The receptionist sounded distressed. He wanted to know how I had booked the room, whether this was the hotel I had booked, how long I was staying and all the rest. Pretty soon it dawned on me that this might be the best bargain I never had. Full of apologies he confirmed that there had been a mistake. I was in the wrong place, and should I want to stay I would have to cough up two hundred more dollars for the privilege. Quite a dent in my tight budget. I scrambled through the room to quickly repack all my belongings, some of them still dripping wet, in order to make a 'complimentary' exit. My personal tuk tuk rider came back to my rescue, patiently waiting outside the front gate. I begged him to take me anywhere else and an alternative accommodation was found nearby.

- Kandy, SRI LANKA -

After the reservation blunder I had just enough time left to visit the Temple of the Tooth Relic, where allegedly a tooth belonging to the Buddha is held. It was the eve of a National holiday and an auspicious full moon day too; crowds were overwhelming. Crammed inside in a sweltering heat, we all waited for the evening puja, when the casket containing the treasure is displayed. Needless to say, spotting a tooth in a rowdy candlelit room was a complete act of faith.

I had grown in strength. From Kandy to Nuwara Eliya I would need it all and more. Starting from the old capital the ride was all the way up to almost two thousand metres, moving from rice fields to tea plantations. A large signpost on the roadside confirmed this.

It read:

'If man has no tea in him, he is incapable of understanding truth and beauty.'

Prepared for a long day, in the early hours of a hot February morning, I began crossing the city. Streets were half asleep and without much traffic, dogs thrived. All taming techniques failed in Kandy. I was chased several times until I decided to radically change my game plan. Something else was suggested to me, a little risky and counter-intuitive. It involved slowing down to walking speed each time I spotted any signs of aggression or imminent attack. As a gesture of goodwill I would first ring my bicycle bell, declare all my good intentions and smile. Taking all that spinning out of the equation, I wasn't an enticing prey anymore and they lost any interest in me.

The road started to rise as bright green rice fields gradually gave way to the darker tones of tea. Literally mountains of them. Every plantation had its own imposing colonial house, reminiscent of past grand style and Cool Britannia. Cycling up the mountain in this heat involved lots of stops. I drank a quarter of a coconut tree and stopped for countless sweet breads and Milo, a chocolate and milk drink I was growing fond of. I spotted a lady cooking coconut flat breads by the side of the road. Just baked, they tasted ever so good. She realised I was Italian and started a long chain of phone calls around family members. Eventually she stuck her mobile phone to my ear as an Italian speaking relative introduced me to yet another migration story. It was most kind of them and I was pleased to be able to put a smile on their faces. After a long crawl up the mountain, it was just a short dive down into Nuwara Eliya.

I reached the guest house and was shown around by a gentle host who introduced himself as 'Neil'. As he pointed out, not his real name but rather a considerate way to spare foreigners from any attempt to pronounce, let alone remember, his tongue-twisting Sinhalese name. A keen cyclist himself, he knew all the backroads on the island and was determined to help me plan the rest of my days. He started to generously pour cup after cup of coffee, and after one hour of unfolding maps and phone calls to reserve rooms he was still going strong.

Nothing would have stopped him had I not felt the urge to mention that I badly needed some food.

The following day at five sharp the morning chanting contest began. The guest house, nested on a steep hill, was blessed by a neighbouring Buddhist temple and mosque. Imam and monks had woken up perky. The night silence was shattered, replaced by chants and bells amplified by loudspeakers for the hearing impaired. After a solid hour it fell back to silence, they must have called a truce and settled on an amicable tie. Despite past tensions, now Sri Lanka offered a wonderful example of Buddhists, Muslims, Christians, and Hindus peacefully mingling and sharing their lives together.

I spotted an exquisite temple where two young novices and a old monk invited me in, eager to show me their secret world. Doors were unlocked and we entered a couple of small rooms with intricately coloured tiled floors and decorated walls. At the centre of it all, the ever present image of a serene Buddha, shiny and gold. I reached Ella in good time and went straight into the usual routine of sightseeing, tropical fruit juices and food. The tiny village was perched up on a lush mountain ridge. It was popular with backpacking westerners and followers of a new-age trail. I walked up a steep, narrow path and checked into a wooden cabin, looking forward to some peaceful rest. I discovered instead how lively and noisy a night in the forest can be. I had only been warned about mischievous monkeys, which in fact were never to be seen. My bedroom was set in the midst of a bird sanctuary, a twitcher's paradise.

For most of the night an eloquent bird I named 'faulty metronome', burst out into loud, out of sync 'tik tok' sounds. He would get regular replies in a completely different tongue. Something like a 'chiii chiii' or along those lines. I wished they would come to a sort of agreement, shut up their beaks and let me sleep.

- Ella, SRI LANKA -

Adventures often start where plans fall apart. Neil had recommended I should take a shortcut via a secondary road from Ella to the village of Haputale, a ride that should have taken me two hours at most. The stubborn side in me decided I should visit Rowena waterfalls instead, seven kilometres down a different road. I thought I should go there first before coming back the same way uphill to follow his original advice. Down I went, on a descent that became steeper and steeper. By the time I reached the waterfalls I knew there was no chance of ever returning back up. I remembered Neil saying this way was long and hard but I decided to believe a tuk tuk driver instead. I asked whether it was long and steep.

"Not really." was the answer.

"You will go down just a little further and then gently rise back up to Haputale."

My experience should have taught me to take such advice with a pinch of salt but I wanted to believe in downhills first. Whether a road goes flat, up or down is irrelevant when riding a tuk tuk; all it takes is a soft roll of the wrist after all. Cyclists are much more sensitive to inclines, much more gravitas is given to grades. I found myself on an unplanned route at the mercy of motorbike riders, passersby and whoever else wished to mislead me further. The more I asked, the more the distances and heights became a matter of personal opinion. Feet and meters got entangled and depending whom I asked, the village of Haputale ranged from a mighty height of 5000 metres to a mere 1200. Distances were even more mysterious.

"How long is it to Haputale?"

"Forty kilometres sir."

The tuk tuk rider's answer was quick and unwavering. It commanded a certain authority. I rode about twenty and asked again, finding out to my surprise that Haputale was still forty kilometres away. Incredibly, the little village was not only moving away from me but it was doing so at my exact speed.

The road was marked as an 'A' road on the map, meaning a major connecting road of the island. In reality it was just a narrow mess, waving up and down through a thick forest, seemingly leading nowhere. The tarmac, when there was something left that is, had the consistency of chewing gum and was melting under the intense heat.

Neil was right. This road was long and challenging, but one thing he got wrong was the amazing scenery. It climbed the edge of the mountain and for hours I could look down to my left where the sloping mountains offered glimpses of the ocean two hundred kilometres away. Without even knowing it I had stumbled into Diyaluma Falls: I later found out it was the second highest in the country dropping from over 600 feet. The intended short ride turned into a very long day. Haputale was getting further and further away the more people I asked. I started to doubt if I would ever make it in daylight and took the wise decision to fold up my bike and get a tuk tuk to take me the remaining seven or twenty eight kilometres, depending on whom you asked. A few minutes later a mighty thunderstorm struck, turning the road into a gushing river. I couldn't help but smile as I sped up the final stretch of a steep road, on board my benevolent three-wheeled saviour.

The following morning I set off in a landscape shrouded in mist, every so often uncovering breathtaking views. The clouds of yesterday's storm were still lingering, and were now broken up into all kinds of shapes. I freewheeled all the way down, heading towards the city of Ratnapura. While crossing the town of Beragala, I noticed a bank and thought I should change some money for the rest of my stay. I parked Bronte right by the entrance, triggering a quick reaction from a stern security guard. He must have thought I had come all the way to Sri Lanka to do a cycling robbery. He approached me embracing his rifle, and told me I couldn't possibly leave my bike parked right at the front of a bank. I said I just needed to quickly change some money at which point he must have realised I wasn't a miscreant. He mellowed and escorted me inside the crowded lobby, leading me right to the front of a long queue of people who were patiently waiting for their turn.

"I will keep an eye on your bike sir. Do not worry."

A foreigner changing currency at Beragala People's Bank was quite an event.

"Sit down sir." said the cashier nervously, as a small crowd gathered all around me.

She stared at my twenty pound notes, disappearing into a back office for what I could only imagine to be a Google search scramble, trying to find out what currency it was and whether it was fake. As the intelligence continued its forensic work, my cashier returned empty handed to her post and started dealing with the rest of the crowd. I sat awaiting some verdict.

"Can we see your passport sir?"

For ten minutes that disappeared too, while withdrawals, cheque deposits and mortgage payments continued to my left and right. Next it was deemed necessary for me to write down my address on a piece of paper. The investigative team finally emerged and put my small bundle of twenty pound notes to further visual and tactile tests.

The proof seemed sound. After a long suspense, there was a general sigh of relief in the bank lobby, they were indeed authentic British pound notes. What I thought would be a quick transaction had taken half an hour or so. I anxiously checked if the armed officer was doing his job ensuring that nobody walked away with my unlocked bike. The transactions around me came to a halt and I was presented with a thick wallop of Rupees that everybody including me started to count, making sure they were right. I had so far only met the most generous and honest of people, but with half the village knowing that I was setting off with a hefty monthly wage on a bike, I dashed out the front door, speeding fast downhill.

Riding fast I couldn't live up to my mission of pleasing the crowds with smiles and English language drills. When riding uphill I was slow and I could manage to answer a comprehensive set of questions such as "hi", "where you going", "which country?", "where's your wife?", "you have children?", "you like Sri Lanka?", "bye". Today all they could get away with was a "hi...bye" sequence at which point I had already zoomed past to a distant horizon.

There was yet another large downpour, but I didn't mind getting soaked every now and then. It had been sunny and very hot, besides rain here was just at the right temperature to be enjoyed. In a light drizzle, I continued my progress to Ratnapura where, after some searching, I was able to locate the secluded Deer Park guest house. Mr Gunawardene offered me a cup of tea and invited me to a home-cooked banquet, cooked by his wife. She turned out to be an excellent cook. The frequent power cuts, plunging the house into total darkness, didn't stop her from producing one of the best meals so far. All ingredients carefully peeled, cut and stir fried under the faint light of multiple candles.

My tour of the Land of Smiles had almost come to an end. The final stretch back to the capital Colombo was much more than the boring transfer I had imagined. For at least half of the way, the road twisted through forested hills, following the Kalu Ganga river as it wound its way to the ocean. In the airline world, the term ditching is used to define an emergency landing on water. As I approached the large city and its increasing traffic, ditching's meaning was much more literal. It involved a humbling diversion into the side bank of the road each time I spotted a large truck coming towards me and heard another one approaching from behind. The hooting would start to grow into a crescendo and I knew it was time to get out of the way. Reaching the outskirts of the capital, it was time to call it a day. I sat by a fruit stall savouring my last, sweet watermelon. I then folded the bike up and hired a tuk tuk, letting local wisdom do the final dangerous driving into the city.

It was time to explore Colombo, usually not the best part of a Sri Lanka sightseeing tour. I enjoyed the evening strolls through the Gangaramaya Temple and the ocean sunset on the long sandy beach, but it otherwise seemed a city trying to win a Nobel prize in chaos. The last memorable experience of this trip came that night. After spending the evening in the city centre a tuk tuk driver offered his services for the long journey back to the suburbs of my guest house. Everywhere else, where traffic is tame and follows written rules, my man would have long been banned from driving anything on wheels. That night, in Colombo's atrocious traffic jam, he was nothing short of a hero. In the half hour it took him to get me back, he drove as if possessed by the devil. Continuously hooting his horn, he spanned all lanes, overtaking cars, trucks and buses like a gifted maniac. Countless times I braced myself and closed my eyes, thinking the end had come. As for him, he was always in control, calm, fearless and totally unperturbed.

Sri Lanka had been a wonderful setting for this cycling adventure. Perfect it was certainly not. I haven't mentioned the polluted cities, the garbage along the roads and the conditions of poverty and squalor far too many people still endured. Yet all that blurred into the background, leaving the kindness and contentment of its people and the children's smiles imprinted on my soul.

- Colombo, SRI LANKA -

* * *

ROCKIES AND BEARS

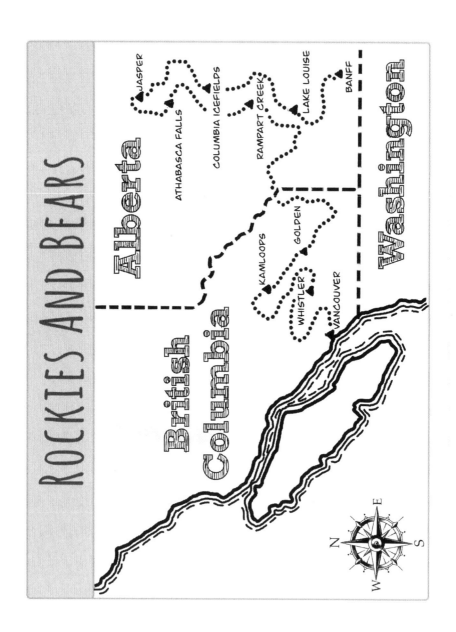

Rockies And Bears

I landed in Calgary Alberta where Air Canada threw in some spice by messing up Bronte's rack. It had been squashed and was preventing the rear wheel from spinning. For once I had decided to trust the look of an intact box and happily boarded a bus heading to Banff. The shuttle took me right to the front door of the Alpine Centre where I had booked my stay. My chirpy disposition, despite the marvellous sights of the unspoilt mountain landscape, was somehow dampened. Assembling my bike and sorting my gear bathed in the sun, I assessed the damage. A rescue plan was needed. The following morning I was back in a rainy Calgary, where I hoped a suitable bike shop, might bestow some good tender loving care on a crooked Bronte.

Justin, the shop repairman, understood my grief and started checking the bike immediately. The bad news was that he didn't have a replacement for two more days but the good news was that with some brute force and a few well applied pulls and pushes, he got the twisted rack back into a decent shape.

"Will I make it to Vancouver?" I asked.

"You should be able to make it..." Justin nodded.

I thanked him for his optimism and help and boarded a bus back to Lake Louise, eager to finally make a start.

The hiccup made the first day of cycling even sweeter. Early morning, under a clear blue sky, I left Lake Louise and entered the Icefields Parkway.

- Lake Louise, Alberta, CANADA -

A good friend had recommended it as one of the most scenic roads on the planet. Completed in 1940, it connects Banff and Jasper National Park, 240 kilometres of glaciers, waterfalls and unspoilt wilderness. Right at the entrance I was welcomed by a large signpost depicting a fat grizzly bear. The small print informed me that there were a lot and recommended I stayed in my vehicle should I encounter one. I didn't have any vehicle to stay in... I decided to let my presence known at all times, discovering how hard it is to cycle up a mountain while whistling and singing. The most pristine and uncontaminated environment was growing wilder by the mile, a grandiose display of breathtaking views. Vast expanses of pine and spruce forests interrupted by dramatic, vertical granite peaks, waterfalls and fast gushing creeks; every now and then, small lakes the colour of jade appeared like scattered gemstones set on a precious ring.

It was July, the height of the summer season, yet traffic was sparse; early morning starts meant I was riding long stretches in total solitude and silence, as if I owned the road. I had planned a stay at the Rampart Creek campsite but as it happened it had just been closed due to a 'bear issue'. The previous morning a grizzly, attracted by some kind of scent, had decided to walk right into a tent, luckily when nobody was around. Nearby was Rampart Creek hostel, a more secure option with walls and doors I could lock. The host Melanie showed me my cosy bed in one of the wooden cabins and brought tears of joy to my eyes, telling me that the little hut I could see up the hill was a natural sauna I was free to use.

The blissmeter reached its peak. I quickly sorted my things and dived into the shack, armed with a box of matches, eager to light up the heap of logs that had been neatly prepared. The crackling fire worked its wonders; the extra large pan, filled with water to the brim, turned lukewarm then piping hot; ladle by ladle I doused away fatigue and sweat, warming up body and soul. It was now time to rest on the wooden bench, pouring the remaining water over the smouldering rocks set on top of the stove; violent spouts of hot steam filled the cabin. It was the best sauna I could have ever had. Bronte had survived its first riding day and restored my hopes that it would keep holding along this magic road.

I was riding the best part of the Icefields Parkway under a warm, shining sun and a clear blue sky. Views were never ordinary and the further north I travelled the more they turned unspoilt and raw. I climbed up to two thousand metres, pushed on by the sheer beauty of my surroundings. I reached the Icefields Centre, one of the few signs of civilisation along the way. It faced glaciers and icefalls and its souvenir shop and restaurant were a magnet for the tourist buses that converged here. The silent mountains I had been riding through were filled with the noise and laughter of Chinese tourists taking a break and sipping instant noodles. I couldn't wait to get out and ride back to peace. I reached Honeymoon Lake campground and while cycling through the entrance gate, a girl on a racing bike was energetically waving at me.

- Athabasca Falls, Alberta, CANADA -

It was the Chinese girl that I had met at Banff hostel. She had told me she was about to join a group cycling tour, riding racing bikes from Jasper to Banff, while I was staring at my wrecked bike, not at all sure I would be able to start mine. I would soon reach Jasper and complete the northbound section of the Icefields Parkway before turning around, heading back south on what felt like the start of another journey, from Jasper to Vancouver. I normally would not have chosen the same road in reverse but with the unpredictable weather in these mountains, it doubled my chances of being able to appreciate it to the full.

I stopped at Athabasca Falls, quite impressive were it not for the fact that I had to fight for a view through a Chinese army of selfie sticks. Fleeing the battle ground, the sky turned the colour of lead and a heavy storm surprised me with nowhere in sight to be able to hide. Resigned to getting soaked, I pulled out all my waterproof gear and faced the rain. I made it to Jasper early and drenched. I entered what seemed, at the time, the best launderette on earth, a paradise for the worn out cyclist. Laundry facilities, three shower rooms, wifi, plugs to recharge gadgets and a café were some of the services on offer. I spent a joyful hour, resetting to a presentable state. A shaven, washed and odourless cyclist was returned to the roads of Alberta. After three days on peanut butter sandwiches, I indulged in an extra large pizza and a rich salad. It was nothing fancy but it felt like a luxurious banquet. I had planned to stay at Whistler campsite but, wary of getting soaked again, I booked the last bed available at the hostel instead. The smell of thunder hung in the air. I arrived just in time to take cover from rain that pelted down in buckets. I congratulated myself, imagining what would have been my fate had I camped instead.

I woke up to a chilly morning in Jasper. Chatting with a guy from Seskatchwan, I discovered the dire state of Canadian railways. He had arrived the previous day, surviving a ghastly delayed train journey. His train took eighteen hours to cover hardly 900 kilometres. He was very philosophical about the whole experience and looked at the positive side of things.

"It was pretty good in the end." he said.

"Halfway through, as we were all starving, they even gave us free meals."

It sounded quite an ordeal, but hearing his accounts gave me another perspective on the distances involved in such a vast, mostly uninhabited country.

In Jasper Route 93 splits into two; for the return leg of the journey, I decided to add some variation and steer on the much quieter 93A. It was a nice detour on a much quieter road. I cycled and sang ever louder for about an hour without crossing a soul, before rejoining the main road. Despite being the middle of July, I was clad in a winter jacket, gloves and woolly hat. The sky looked threatening once again. At Sunwapta Falls, the only opportunity for a decent meal that day, I walked into the restaurant as rain started falling. I indulged in a high calories meal like a camel storing fat in his hump. Meal and refills lasted enough for the seasons to change and for a warm sun to return and shine. Heavy, I struggled up the first climbs, finally reaching Beauty Creek where I met Theo, a girl from Atlanta. She was cycling Banff to Jasper on her first ever solo bike trip. An unsociable and ever vanishing host checked us in and informed us, with a hint of sadness, that it would have been a full dorm that night.

Theo and I had a quiet dinner, sharing cycling stories in the very basic kitchen hut. Being off the grid, all 'appliances' in order to work, needed a clockwise or anti-clockwise twist of a particular valve connected to a gas bottle or generator; given the evanescent nature of the manager, and the explosive nature of things, a user manual seemed badly needed. As the evening approached it was still only the two of us and we were wondering what had happened to the crowds that were meant to be descending on such a remote corner. As the tired cyclists hit the sack ready for a well deserved night's sleep, it all came suddenly to life. The large party arrived and in a clumsy to-ing and fro-ing, began to conquer unfamiliar bunk beds navigating around hidden corners. The pitch black dorm was lit in bursts by flashing headlamps, painting cast shadows on the bare white walls. All trampling and clatter settled and left me wondering whether it had just been a bad dream.

By the morning there were low clouds and a steady drizzle. I headed to the kitchen hut for breakfast, eager to figure out what all the buzz at Beauty Creek was about. A group of hikers from Edmonton had taken total possession of the kitchen. Large cool boxes filled every empty corner in the room. They were packed to the brim with assorted food in what looked like a base camp preparation for a summit attempt on mount Everest. They were staying for three nights and had planned to do daily treks, hiking the local trails. One by one, more and more people trickled into the room, rain somehow dampening their enthusiasm.

- Columbia Icefields, Alberta, CANADA -

To cheer up they turned to cakes, fried sausages, bacon and eggs; Theo and I were eager to join in, putting our cycling appetites to test. By nine o'clock the sky got lighter, spurring last minute preparations and packing. We wished each other good luck and I set off under a light drizzle, for an uphill climb to Columbia Icefields. The road from the opposite side offered fresh perspectives, and heading south meant that, should it ever appear, I would have the sun in my face for most of the day.

Alan and Melanie were pleased to welcome me once again at Rampart Creek. Melanie told me she had crossed me on the road a few hours earlier, while driving.

"You had such a beaming smile on your face..." she said.
"If that is how it feels like being on a cycling tour, I should go on one myself."

Trained on my previous stay, it was soon time to take the lead and get the sauna ready by lighting the fire. We spent the rest of the evening around a bonfire, chatting and eating 'smors', marshmallows and chocolate sandwiches skewered and roasted over the charcoals and flames.

For the first time in Canada, there were faint hints of summer. The spectacular views of Saskatchewan Crossing, where the river spread its tentacles of rivulets, were scarred by the darkened frames of pine trees, recent victims of a forest fire. It was the prelude of a series of steep hills that felt very different from the time I had enjoyed them downhill. Once on top I glided down the mountain, staring at the beauty and incredible colours of Bow and Waterfowl lake.

It took six days to get back to Lake Louise and complete the Icefields Parkway loop. Bronte had rolled on admirably, the rack seemingly holding in place. A little more confidence to now start heading west. I checked into the large campsite and was soon joined by Sophie, a student from Minneapolis. A few days before she had set off by herself with car and tent and, despite having just crossed the border, she had already run out of Canadian dollars. She asked whether she would be able to share my site, which was not a problem. Space was never an issue in Canada and camping spots were far larger than needed, unless one was planning to start farming.

It was still bright and in the early afternoon I headed up to the lake that gives the name to this famous skiing resort. It was another lapis lazuli jewel, cast deep among steep rising rock faces. To the side stood the luxurious Fairmont Hotel in all its majesty. By now I had seen quite a few such lakes. Impressive as it was, this one was a little too tamed and congested by pampered crowds. The traffic down the narrow road was atrocious but Bronte's advantage in this situation was obvious. I sped down fast past everyone's frustration of getting nowhere.

I thanked Alberta for taking good care of me and joined the Trans-Canada highway. Completed in 1971, it was at the time the longest uninterrupted highway in the world. Luckily most of it seemed to have a safe enough emergency lane that I could use with my bike. Approaching Golden, the road climbed up a hill and abruptly turned into a narrow one lane with no shoulder. I had a reminder of how fragile life can sometimes be. I was creeping up the hill when I heard a truck approaching from behind, the driver determined to overtake me despite the lack of space. I steadied my nerves going as straight as I could on a razor thin line between the vehicle and the rock face. The metal monster brushed past me, so close that I could spot the tense driver's face reflected on the side mirror. They felt the longest few seconds of my life but in the end I was spared. In Field, I celebrated my lucky escape with a sweet cheese cake and a coffee. The ranger that had checked me in at Lake Louise campsite was sitting at a nearby table with two other friends. We introduced ourselves; his name was Takeshi and like Mina, his girlfriend, he was born in Japan but had lived most of his life in Canada. I surprised them by producing some of my most elegant Japanese.

Crossing into British Columbia and Yoho National Park I had a weird urge to search for a Canadian registration plate among the plastic bottles and garbage thrown by the side of the road. I quickly turned into an efficient 'plate spotter'.

With practice, plates seemed to spring up all over the place, like mushrooms after an autumn rain. The addiction began as I spotted an Alberta registration plate and picked it up thinking it would make a nice gift for Bronte. Not much further I recognised a British Columbia one too, it looked battered and dusty. The new pastime was getting out of control, it slowed me down too much and gave me a sore neck. If I kept at it I would soon be squashed under the weight of a pile of tin. I cycled past it but like any addiction, the itch just grew. I walked back, crossed the road barrier and dived into the ditch, picking it up. To my astonishment it turned out to be a one off gem; A British Columbia plate, registration '1 Bike'. Unaware of the reasons why it had ended up there, I gave it new life and hung it right at the front of my bike. Bronte was now fully registered and on its way to Vancouver.

On my longest cycling day I had the pretence to include a climb up the 1330 metres of Rogers Pass. I left early in the morning under torrential rain and the darkest of skies right where I was heading. Any resident of the British Isles confronts rain with resilience, and a 'one is not a lump of sugar' kind of way. I faced the elements until the day turned completely around and I was baking under a scorching sun. Canadians take their National Parks very seriously. The noble effort to not leave any human trace and risk spoiling their pristine nature, results in a total lack of the most basic facilities. Tourists were desperately seeking the simplest of pleasures, deprived of any signs of edible food, a water tap or the privacy of a restroom. Cyclists, the least polluting lot, had been completely forgotten. I was running thirsty and after a vain search for a faucet, I had to finally surrender and resort to begging car drivers for a spare water bottle or two. Online maps were not perfect after all. Detailed internet searches and planning had presumed that a dot and a name meant some kind of civilised community. This was not the case and more often than not they remained mysterious dots on an uninhabited land.

What I had lost in hydration, I gained in time instead. I crossed the timeline between Rocky Mountain Time and Pacific Time. In an instant I gained an extra hour of life on a bicycle . The event was marked by an ordinary little road sign that I think only Bronte and I were slow enough to see. Tested by the long day, I reached Canyon Hot Springs.

Research and planning had informed me that there was a decent campground here at which to spend the night. There was further advice and warnings. The Chinese owner was so fond of sprinklers that the dry land was regularly flooded and turned into a swamp. Reviews unanimously agreed: the trick was to ask for a spot that Mr Chan's sprinklers were not able to reach. My site luckily was beyond the limits of his longest hosepipes and his efforts to keep the lawn lush and green in the middle of a summer drought. Here, the summer had been particularly dry and our hero was feeling the strain. He frantically spent his days driving a golf cart hither and thither, shifting entangled hoses and strategically positioning sprinklers like pawns ready to give checkmate.

Other warnings concerned his eagerness to charge for everything but the air one breathed. To fine tune his control, plastic tokens were the current currency at Canyon Hot Springs. Chan's dollars were needed to use most facilities. Entering the shop front door had to be done by a synchronised sprint, timed with the brief instants when sprinklers aimed elsewhere. No wonder, the lack of any competition within hundreds of miles meant that everything was expensive. I left short on food but loaded with tokens as if about to win a Monopoly contest.

Before dusk all taps were shut off and sprinklers were given a deserved rest. After a decent night's sleep, by seven thirty the following morning the tent was dismantled, Bronte was loaded up and ready to charge further. At the campground exit I met a German cyclist couple that I had seen arrive the previous day. They were traveling in style and had reserved one of the luxurious wooden cabins that lined the main campsite access way. These looked idyllic and, needless to say, cost a lot of Chan's dollars. Despite their cosy appearance, hidden right in their backyard and inches away, were the rails of the Trans Canadian Railway. Our enterprising owner had transformed the old station and platform into chalets and balconies, a trainspotter's paradise. The Canadian Trans Pacific railway is a constant presence along Highway one; the two meet and part as if playing hide and seek. When out of sight, slow endless trains can be heard hooting their horns during the day as well as at the most ungodly hours of the night. The German couple, having checked in on platform one, had endured a rough night indeed and were not up to small talk. Their eye bags hanging low on their cheeks told stories of a troublesome night.

"Did you sleep well?" they asked.

"Very well indeed. And you?"

"Not too bad." was the quick reply, pursed lips restraining the will to curse.

"We could hear the trains a little..."

I passed Revelstoke, or Revy as it was endearingly called by locals. A picturesque little town where, unlike in the National Parks, a good latte and freshly baked bread seemed never too far away. The road gently descended, coasting a series of small lakes. I stopped at Three Rivers lake, and spotting some kids swimming was too much of a temptation to resist. It was summer after all, and I didn't want to let these northern latitudes prevent me from taking a quick dip.

- Mount Sir Donald, British Columbia, CANADA -

It had been a much more relaxing day, I hadn't risked my life and could peacefully check in at Yard Creek Provincial Park where the hosts Bob and Sandy welcomed me.

As well as registration plates, I had also acquired a certain fondness for flag patches. I had bought a Canadian flag patch, planning to transform my Vietcong wide brimmed hat into something a little less controversial. Sandy was very enthusiastic and eager to offer her stitching skills and cover the blight of that communist red star. She disappeared in her caravan with hat and Canadian badge, determined to put things right. She reappeared rather too quickly, a large grin announcing the successful completion of the task. Unless I had just met a stitching speed champion, my perfectionist side had good reason to be concerned. She returned the hat with her haphazard stitches and entangled threads. I had to pull out an Oscar winning performance, praising her precise work while I couldn't help but notice the mess she had made.

Before bedtime I turned on the radio eager to catch up with the world and a bit of Canadian Broadcasting news. The topic of the night involved a heated debate on the plight of the million American birds, crashing each year into cities' skyscrapers. It was a gruesome state of affairs. A distressed 'Bird Collision Campaign Manager' called in live, unloading a mighty rant on the evils of glass transparency. She pleaded for more sensitivity and for windows to be made opaque.

Canada is a vast and sparsely populated country. Solitude brings good will and an eagerness to help, as I found out after my first and, I hoped, last flat tyre of the trip. I pulled to the side of the road onto a wooden bridge and started removing my rear wheel in order to fix it. In the time it took to repair Bronte, no driver failed to stop and offer help, water or a tempting ride to the next town. Delayed by the puncture, I arrived at the Shuswap hostel in Squilax, undoubtedly the most interesting place I had ever stayed in. I had booked a bunk bed in what was called a "caboose". After a friendly check-in at the reception desk set inside a grocery store, I was escorted up and down flights of steps and tight corridors into the back yard. I was in a fairytale. We walked our way past chubby rabbits and grazing lamas before entering another building; finally we reached the garden by the lake where, in an engineering feat, stood four old Canadian Pacific sleeper carriages. After complaining about trains waking me up at night, for once I had to be grateful that one of them had been silenced and tamed.

The following day started with three hearty pancakes with maple syrup personally cooked by Blair, the remarkable host.

How could anybody not be in awe?

One day she had woken up with the idea of buying four old rail carriages - she had them delivered to her back garden and turned them into a functioning hostel. She was full of life and charm. Once breakfast was over she insisted I should use her kayak and roam the lake too.

Regretfully I had to decline for lack of time. I followed the Thompson river, heading towards Kamloops. As the large town approached, the quiet road turned into a three lane motorway where cycling was banned. I couldn't find any alternative way, but after all the warnings and past memories of a police chase in San Francisco, I thought it best to stop by a local bicycle shop and ask.

"Is it true that I can't cycle along the highway?" I asked.

"That's right..." was the unanimous chorus.

"There isn't any other road around here," I said with some frustration.

"How is one supposed to get to Vancouver?"

I had touched a sensitive spot in the local cycling community. There was a synchronised shrugging of shoulders, followed by some expletives and the most unkind words aimed at Kamloops Traffic Police department.

"Just ignore those signs and pedal on!"

Those were the only words I wanted to hear. I charged on, against the law, a cycling revolutionary of sorts. As I crossed the city, I veered off the main highway, turning north instead, following the much quieter and scenic highway 97. The landscape turned into a Canada I didn't know; a few turns around the hills uncovered a desert-like landscape, surrounding Kamloops Lake. What was meant to be a short day staying in Kamloops ended in Savona instead, turning into the longest ride Bronte and I had ever done. What a bike! Bronte would surprise even more the following day when I ended up covering 128 kilometres of breathtaking dry lands, reaching the little town of Lillooet. I spotted the first few signposts to Vancouver too; a few more days and this adventure would come to an end.

I had more to look forward to - Whistler, a recent Winter Olympics host - before descending for another glimpse of the Pacific Coast before reaching the city itself.

Before reaching the steepest ascent yet, I was hoping for an early and restful night at Lillooet campground. Everybody else seemed to have other plans; loud speakers blasted beat after beat of thumping music late into the night. I nursed my sore legs, my tent pitched in the middle of a rave party. The troubled night turned into a morning fiasco. At four o'clock the campsite came to life with the hustle and bustle of a crowd hastily dismantling tents and starting their noisy engines. A little later it was back to total silence. I unzipped my tent. The packed campsite of the night before was now almost empty, only a few tents left standing. Had the biblical Apocalypse just begun? Searching for some answers over a hefty breakfast in a high street café, I realised that this was not going to be an ordinary day in Lillooet. By luck, or lack of it, I had arrived on the exact day of the Sturgeon Derby, the most important event of the year. A day later, laughing, I spotted headlines in the local newspapers:

'With a catch measuring seven feet, five-and-a-half inches, James Zucchelli earned the bragging rights at the Winners Edge 12th Annual Sturgeon Derby. Zucchelli landed the giant fish around 7 a.m. July 26th at the Butchers Hole on the Fraser River before returning it to the river in the catch-and-release event. He was very careful to hold the fish properly and keep much of the sturgeon's body in the river while photos were taken. It was a long 50 minutes of struggle to land the sturgeon he later said, but every minute was well worth it.'

Good for him.

One thing had been clear from the start of this journey: Duffey Lake Road would be the harshest of them all. A long, narrow strip of road relentlessly climbing up steep grades. I dreaded the prospect of having to cycle, or rather walk it, but if I was to make it to the coast there was no other option. After two weeks and a thousand kilometres, I certainly didn't lack stamina and willingness to endure pain. A strong headwind made it a really tough hurdle. After four hours of painfully slow cycling, a few walks and some colourful cursing, I finally reached the top. Celebrations were cut short, dampened by a sudden thunderstorm. The quick drop in temperature made me decide I should keep pedalling fast down the other side. Heavy rain continued for all the descent and only stopped before Pemberton when the sun began to shine. Luckily, body and soul were pretty dry before reaching and setting up camp at Nairn Falls provincial Park where I was about to unwittingly stumble into another major event. The following day was a big day in Whistler as the Ironman competition would take over the place. This meant having to start my cycling early, trying to reach Whistler before all roads were closed.

The following day was not meant for any outdoor activity. I packed my tent just in time to keep it dry but from then up to Whistler things turned extremely gloomy. Being in the mountains it was freezing cold too. What kept me positive and riding was seeing those poor triathletes cycling up the frosty mountain in their tight thin swimsuits. It was not called Whistler Ironman for nothing; distances to be covered bordered lunacy. Who was I to complain when this lot was setting off for a 180 kilometres of cycling, 5 kilometres of swimming in an icy lake and a full marathon too? Dripping and frozen, I didn't present my best self at the information centre in Whistler. I had to steady my nerves on being told that the hostel I had reserved was not in the village but in fact a mere eight kilometres further on under pouring rain. The gentlest remark I could utter was 'you must be joking...'

They weren't, it was nothing but the plain truth and I didn't want to hear it. Once I reached the hostel, misery levels were greatly reduced. It was modern and comfortable, built as accommodation for the 2010 Winter Olympics athletes. A few hours later, with the rain having stopped and a timid sun reappearing, I put Bronte on a bus and returned to the village for a little sightseeing. Whistler was a beautiful place for those who could afford it, a kind of Beverly Hills on ice. As for myself and the rest of the backpacking crowd, it seemed the kind of place where you could only afford to gaze through the windows. It was pay back time on the weather front. A sunny forecast set me off on my last day of cycling, destination the city of Vancouver.

I couldn't wait to descend from the mountains, over forty kilometres to the town of Squamish, reuniting with the Pacific Coast. The first few short glimpses of a narrow inlet led to wider views, the ocean hugging the coast and reminding me of my past Oregon and California rides just further south. I met one of the other few cyclists too, a German girl taking a ferry to Vancouver Island to follow the Sunshine Coast. She described how beautiful it was and certainly gave me a good excuse to return one day. I had always wanted to visit Vancouver.

- Lions Bay, British Columbia, CANADA -

Often at the top of world rankings for the best quality of living, it seemed an ideal place to be spending the last few days of my trip. I cycled slowly to savour each pedal stroke, feeling the breeze gently brush past my face. In a glorious and warm sunshine, I saw the ramps of Lions Gate Bridge, the grand entrance to another beautiful city. Bronte had, once again, taken me far.

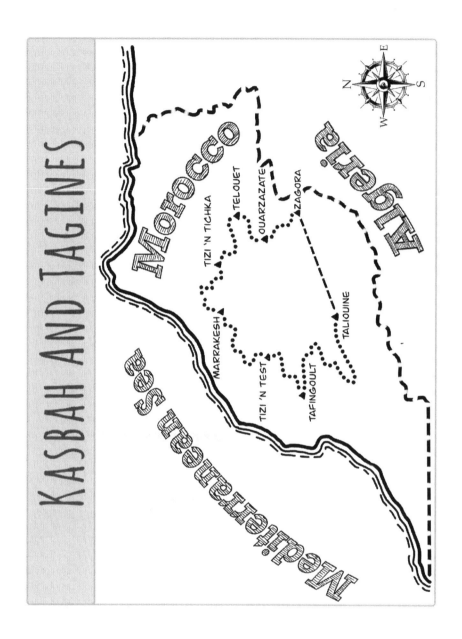

Kasbah and Tagines

T he end of winter had arrived with a Siberian twist bringing snow, blizzards and ice. The evacuation couldn't have been more timely. As an introduction to a new continent Bronte and I opted for some familiarity. African beginners, we thought it best to cling to the edges rather than diving too deep. It was going to be Morocco. Warm and friendly, land of mountains, desert and sea, it had become a popular destination for European cycling adventurers seeking a culture shock close to home. The proposed plan was a loop departing and returning to the walled medieval city of Marrakesh. Starting from the Berber empire medina, with its maze of alleys and souks, it would take in a lot of Atlas Mountains, countless Kasbah, the edge of the Sahara desert and a lot of tagines.

Africa was only three hours away and yet so far. On a late winter Monday all airlines conspired to land at Menara International Airport at the same time and see what would happen. Descending the steps into the large immigration hall we all gasped in horror. Crowds shifted left and right in a haphazard scramble directed by immaculately dressed traffic attendants. Everyone was trying to figure out how to fill in entry cards without a pen. Rumours spread of an imminent German arrival, surely they would come equipped with pens? For at least two hours we joined an aimless queue that seemed to run in a circle. Increasingly familiar faces disappeared into a separate lane to then reappear half an hour later, nowhere nearer an immigration desk. Lasting friendships were built. There were screams here and there too. A man start yelling that he had claustrophobia and was feeling unwell. A skilfully played card indeed, he was paraded right to the front of the mayhem.

- Marrakech, MOROCCO -

The long wait to face immigration and customs was a total let down. A grumpy officer, while hardly looking at my face, thumped down the official stamp.

"Is that all?" I said rather disappointed.

"Can I go?"

He nodded, rather annoyed.

I had almost made it into Morocco were it not for a further set of unexpected checks and x ray scans at customs. Packed bike - all the rest I carried - disappeared down yet another conveyor belt. The officer waved at me, calling me to the other side.

"You have drugs?"

"Well... not that I know of." I said unconvincingly.

Such a question delivered so bluntly left me a little shocked.

Granted my luggage is always a bit unusual, but my outdoorish smart-wear hardly looked the part. Looking at some of the characters around I could safely say that there were better candidates. Bags were opened for inspection. Luckily what had triggered the search were the countless silica sachets I had packed to keep humidity away from my gadgets. I breathed a sigh of relief as the sliding doors opened and I was granted access to Marrakesh. There was much scrambling on the other side too. Here a host of drivers shouted and held up cardboard signs with tourists' names. Youssef my driver had been patiently waiting, unphased by the long delay. I spotted his card reading Riad Si Amarra, amongst all the taxis, buses and private cars jostling for work.

The following morning, I cycled back to the medina in order to finally get some Dirhams, the local currency. Nobody so far had liked my credit cards. The simple act of withdrawing one from my wallet triggered power failures and technical faults of all sorts. Sorry my machine doesn't work...You have euros? I spotted an atm machine and, just as I inserted my card, a character approached begging with great persistence. Not the best thing to happen while waiting to withdraw the equivalent of a good monthly wage. Sorry as I felt for him, I was feeling rather uncomfortable. Hoping he wouldn't try to snatch the bundle and run, I couldn't come up with a lamer excuse than to say that I didn't have any small change.

After a visit to Koutoubia mosque and its gardens, I started cycling along route 203, pointing straight to the mountains. I was soon faced with something that I couldn't explain. The figure of an old and frail man kept appearing in the distance. He was crouching on his rickety bike painfully pushing on his pedals with his flip flops. His progress being excruciatingly slow, I would overtake him with a polite wave.

Hardly thirty minutes later I would have a deja vu, spotting him once again far ahead of me. Each time I caught up with him he would grin at me, his eyes beaming through the pair of thick glasses he was wearing. The intriguing event repeated itself many times, to the point that I got to know his name, Hassan. I was beginning to wonder whether he was a guardian angel of some sort, spurring me safely on. The secret was much more mundane and was revealed when I saw him descending from a pickup van. He must have been a popular chap, and out of generosity every now and then acquaintances stopped to offer him and his bike a lift as far as they could take him.

Out of a blue morning haze the snowy peaks of the Atlas mountains finally revealed themselves. I could spot Mount Toubkal, the highest of them all. Over four thousand metres high, its top was still shrouded in white snow and quite a sight to behold. Each time I stopped to speak to people I found them incredibly friendly and kind. Being particularly bad at remembering names, I liked the fact that everyone was either a Youssuf, an Ali, a Mohammed or an Hassan. I had a tasteful introduction to my first lamb tagine too followed by a long chat with the restaurant owner and some of the other customers sitting on the sunny patio. It was all wonderful and relaxing to the point that I got up and left without feeling I should pay. I had hardly started pedalling when I heard some French being shouted:

"Monsieur, monsieur. L'addition!"

Yussuf was pleading for his due. Still panting, he passed on the card of his brother's hotel on top of Tizi 'n Test pass, my next destination.

Berber salesmanship is something to behold. I was invited to sit down at a café's garden by a large man wearing a white robe, a turquoise turban wrapped around his head. I wanted to drink some mint tea but I had hardly taken my seat when he joined me at my table. After a pleasant chat, a leather display of silver bracelets was unrolled on the table in front of me. Determined to say no, I asked him to stay and have a cup of tea instead. With a look of disappointment on his face he still wouldn't let his sales pitch slacken for a moment, determined to make a sell. He partially succeeded in the end. After such persistence I thought I should give in to a small bracelet that had dropped half of its original value in a matter of a few words.

"You are a good man." he said.

"Thank you." I replied rather puffed.

"...and because you are a good man I will give you this larger bracelet." "Just give me back the other one and for only 200 dirhams more I'll give you this one instead."

I kept pouring more mint tea into his cup hoping to drown some of his eloquence. I worried that in a couple of weeks I would return from these mountains, bracelets dangling the length of my arm. I cycled further up the hill until dusk wrapped the mountains and a perfect tent spot by the Nfis river could be found.

Rivers never sleep, neither did I. The gushing sound not far from my right ear got louder the more I tried to ignore it. In the morning I started to tackle the High Atlas, rising over two thousand metres to Tizi n'Test. The road had been skillfully built in six years by the French in the 1920s. It took me four hours of incessant climbing to reach its top, cycling through a meandering gorge of red and purple rock and sands. The slow progress allowed plenty of time to appreciate the views of deserted valleys and abandoned Kasbahs. Cycling is a learning process and I discovered many other things too. Taking a picture with an old lady standing by her mule cost ten Dirhams, and for larger coins no change was given. In the remote villages they hadn't caught up with my chest mounted camera. I could still discreetly keep filming for free. I made some acquaintance with Moroccan dogs too. They were wiser than their Sri Lankan counterpart. All they did was stare at me with melancholy in their eyes and without any fidgeting, letting me cycle by.

It is always interesting to see the resourcefulness of man in places where there is a lack of services.

In these remote corners of Morocco, every private van or truck becomes part of the public transport system. I regularly spotted vehicles stopping and waiting by the side of the road in the middle of nowhere. A short hooting was all it took to trigger a procession of people hurrying down the mountain trails or scrambling up invisible paths in order to get a lift to the nearest town. Fares I assumed must have been very reasonable too as they made great use of their limited space. When full on the inside there was always space on the roof, and for the most intrepid ones the last available spot was the cheapest bargain of them all. It involved what looked to me like a van crucifixion. The brave man held for dear life, standing squashed on the outside of the rear doors. Arms stretched wide, he held onto the roof rack, the tips of his feet placed on the bumper.

- Ouirgane, MOROCCO -

The valleys turned dryer as I climbed further but here and there were the signs of spring with wild flowers and cherries in full bloom. I stepped up my bargaining skills and was proud of a one third off discount on an omelette. There was still room for improvement though, the old man at the café was still smiling at the end. In Ijoukak I visited the imposing Tin Mal mosque, built in 1153 and a Unesco Heritage site. The gruelling climb eventually led to the top of Tizi'n Test, searching for Mustapha. He appeared beaming with a large smile. His brother had told him a cyclist was on his way and surely warned him I might try to run off without paying the following day. I checked into a room at the top of the Atlas while dark clouds were building up, rising across the mountain ridge and causing the temperature to drop below freezing. Mustapha led me to my room and quickly set alight two portable gas canisters, my heating system for the night.

"Please make sure you turn these off before you fall asleep..." he emphasised with some concern.

What he really meant was that failure to do so would cause a premature death. This was confirmed by several warning notes hanging around the walls. They encouraged guests to be vigilant and follow the same advice. It did warm up slightly, but a nasty smell of gas and a total lack of health and safety spread throughout the room.

Taking a little walk around the entrance I met the other guests. A couple of elderly Germans traveling with a camper van and their dog, as well as a young Moroccan astronomer. He had come a long way, his car filled with all kinds of telescopes and lenses, eager to explore the night sky. Needless to say, the bad weather and unfavourable conditions meant he was pretty upset. In freezing temperatures we were all trembling, wearing anything we could find. We were invited into the only warm room on the premises, which by chance happened to be where the owner lived. Fighting for the closest seat to the fireplace we huddled together and were served a cosy dinner. It was time to get some rest as I warily walked back to my room. By now it was smelling like a proper gas chamber. I turned off the flimsy shutoff valves, praying they wouldn't set off the ticking bombs, and disappeared under a thick pile of blankets.

Everybody survived gas inhalations and frost and saw the light of another day. The sunshine pierced through a thick blanket of fog covering the mountain below. Morocco was still bitterly cold. Guests once again huddled over a hearty breakfast discussing our lucky escapes and the various plans for the day. Energies restored and glowing in my fluorescent yellow rain jacket I dived down the other side of the mountain, disappearing in a milky mist. While coping with an icy drizzle and a perilous descent, a second messenger appeared. This time he turned up in the shape of a chubby cyclist with a northern British accent. He emerged from the opposite direction, moving painfully and slowly up the hill. At first I saw a faint hologram mixed in with the dark thick fog, a faint shadow that slowly gained a more definite contour. He sported a long white beard that flowed around his bicycle handlebar and had collected shiny droplets that trickled down in frosty beads. In true British spirit he was wearing only a pair of thin lycra shorts and a t-shirt, and endured frostbite with a straight face. We exchanged a few words before disappearing in the misery of our respective ways. As I descended further the low clouds eventually lifted, but the road disappeared instead. Ten kilometres of road works had been scheduled to coincide with my arrival. Large signboards advertised the fact that this total mess was necessary to bring Morocco into the twenty-first century. To me old twentieth century tarmac would have done just fine. I crawled at walking pace along the dusty road. reaching the Souss plain and a sparse vegetation of argan trees.

There was an update in prices on the other side of the Atlas. A picture of a Berber shepherd with goats cost 10 Dirham. When running low on small change, you could get a Berber only photograph for 5 Dh. Filming was still free. My camera, clamped to a chest harness and protruding out of my chest, was ready to film at the push of a button. A small red light would start flashing but nobody dared to ask questions and run the risk of being insensitive. For all they knew it could have well been some kind of life saving medical device. As far as road signs went, I was getting a little concerned. Next to Arabic and at times the familiar French,   new unintelligible hieroglyphics had started to appear. I later found out it was Berber and hoped they wouldn't drop my French or I would be completely lost.

Did you know that goats could climb trees?

I certainly didn't and you can imagine my surprise when I spotted a dozen goats clinging to the high branches of a 'goat tree'. It cost me 5 Dirham to convince the Berber shepherd to let me approach them and be allowed to take some pictures of their incredible feat. Strange as it seemed to me, in this part of the world it is simply routine. After half a day of passing by goat trees along the road, the novelty wore off and I hardly paid any notice.

There were some hints of desert as I approached Taliouine, the world's biggest saffron growing area. Together with Argan oil, yet another useless product to the wandering cyclist. Next I had to take a bus transfer, heading east towards Zagora and the Draa Valley. From there I had scheduled a reunion with Menno a Dutch friend and adventurer who would be joining me for the rest of the way. Timetables, carefully researched online, failed miserably. Not only were the departure times wrong, entire journeys didn't exist. My 11:50 service from Tailouine to Zagora was wishful thinking and pure fantasy. The only option was going to Ouarzazate instead, two hundred kilometres north of my target. Half of the crowd waiting at the bus stop got passionately involved in sorting out my plans. Consensus was reached that once in Ouarzazate a further bus trip to Zagora on the same day should not be impossible. I noticed the bus approaching from down the hill and had little time left to make up my mind. I decided I should be dispatched there instead, inshallah. Priority was granted to the panicking tourist and in split seconds a ticket was bought. Bronte was folded and put into a plastic bag with the helpful assistance of passersby. A middle aged man impressed by what he had just seen, asked how much the bike was and whether I would sell it to him. One hundred euros, I said, not wanting to attract too much attention, but no thanks... Bronte was well over ten times that, but priceless to me.

I set off on a four hours journey of sermons and prayers blasted through loudspeakers and a radio faithfully tuned to Prophet fm. The mystic experience was enhanced by the sudden 'Allah Ah Bar' ringtones of mobile phones receiving calls. I was the only foreigner on a packed bus, asking for some 80s classic music instead would have been plain rude. I felt an outsider and was ready to convert. The broadcasted good deeds bore fruit and miraculously my transfer worked out. After two further hours of prayers in Ouarzazate station's mosque, I boarded a connecting bus and reached Zagora by eight o'clock that night. I was now on the border of the Sahara desert, everything getting more and more exotic. I extricated my bike from a mountain of luggage bundles and in the darkness set out through a maze of bustling alleys and streets in search of a guest house. I eventually found Karim Sahara and had a warm welcome by Samir. He upgraded my stay to a larger room with a very hard bed.

Forget New York City, Zagora instead is the city that never sleeps. I came with a messed up body clock, occupational hazard of any long haul airline employee, but Zagora is not for the light sleeper. I had hardly fallen asleep when I was woken up by a crescendo of rumbling drums accompanied by a loud yodeling and loud chanting. I checked the time. It was two o'clock at night and I pinched myself to make sure this was indeed happening. Starved of news for over a week I wondered whether there was a kind of revolt in the streets of Zagora. The kerfuffle seemed to converge and finally settle around my guest house. The neighbourhood was engulfed in drumbeats and shouting, the general commotion gathering pace. I felt like my bed had been gently lowered to the centre pitch of Wembley stadium in the midst of a sell out final. After an hour and a half the rattling stopped, but all that noise had thrown the cockerels out of sync. It was just past three am, their duty to wake up people had been inappropriately usurped and they let it be known by a round of stroppy crowing. We then all enjoyed half an hour of silence and peace. At four thirty loudspeakers were switched on and a pre-call to prayers called all the faithful to the mosque. The call was answered and by five am prayers were in full swing. I gave up trying to get some rest. Over breakfast I met Samir and asked what all the night activities had been about.

"Oh, that was just part of a wedding." he said.

"The bride joins the groom in his family house for the first time."

Surprised by my question, I suppose for him a sleepless night was one of the joys of living in town.

- Draa Valley, MOROCCO -

The further south one travels the cheaper it gets. In Aoulouz a large portion of chicken, beans, some flatbread and a mint tea cost the equivalent of five pictures of an old lady with mule. If I kept traveling south at this rate, I had a theory that soon enough I would get paid to eat instead. Skin complexions, including mine, was getting darker too. I continued my cycling, following the oasis along the Draa Valley to the town of Agdz where the meeting with Menno was scheduled.

Inspired by my travels, and owner of a Brompton folding bike himself, he had decided to give it a try and test it on a few days' ride. I had some worries about the success of his trial. He had mostly cycled on long expeditions and was used to recumbent bikes, trailers and other larger contraptions. Limited space had never been an issue as he could carry the kitchen sink and more. He had a great fondness for gadgets and the tendency to bring along things he would never be able to use. Folding bikes are different. It is all about minimalism, cutting life to basics to limit the weight and hoping that the little wheels will hold in place. Furthermore, Menno is a man of conspicuous size, almost two metres tall with thighs as large as my waist. Getting back to Marrakech demanded a serious change of attitude on his part and a miracle or two.

I met him at the bus stop in Agdz. The twisting journey up and down the Atlas mountains had left his stomach in tatters. On the positive side his bike was in good shape and I was relieved to find out that his belongings had been cut down to size too. Yes, there were a few new gadgets he was eager to show me, but his luggage had gone through some drastic downsizing. That was the spirit, I admired his change of heart.

He joined me for what turned out to be the best part of the trip. This side of the Draa Valley had lost any sign of a river or oasis. What remained was a dry landscape with hardly a village between the towns of Agdz and Ouarzazate. Strong headwinds hit our face all day. It felt like one of those rebel birds on the Pacific Coast that against all odds are determined to fly north. I had watched them flap their wings frantically, their effort just enough to stay still. Inevitably they would give up, realising that south was not bad after all and let the wind do all the carrying. I was flapping my legs but only moved at a snail's pace. I didn't have the freedom and carelessness of a bird. Turning around meant going back to Zagora, and I would never want to risk going through another wedding night. I faced the ultimate cyclist's humiliation and had to pedal hard even down steep descents. As for Menno, he was a Flying Dutchman that nothing could have stopped. Born and bred in flat Holland, he rode like a monster on small wheels, climbing mountains like a goat. Just shy of his sixties, his fitness level was astounding and I rode behind him most of the time. We were offered great views and no effort was in vain.

Reading accounts of other cyclists' adventures in Morocco gave me the idea to bring small gifts. Pens seemed to be a popular choice for children they met along the way. Trying to be original, I brought a series of Japanese assorted stickers instead. Kids were not impressed.

"Monsieur vous avez un stylo?" Do you have a pen? they would ask.

They reminded me of the time I also so much wanted a pen to fill out entry cards at Marrakesh airport.

"Pens? No, sorry. I am still looking for one myself."

"What about a nice Japanese sticker instead?"

They resigned themselves to it, but I could detect some disappointment on their faces. It was a vicious circle. Tourists brought pens to children who asked for pens because they knew that tourists might have them.

One morning I woke up with a jolt. I could hear a voice shouting 'Get up! Get up! Get up!' Half out of my bed, following the commands, I realised it was just an alarm ringtone. Menno had downloaded a US

Army sergeant major app, bullying young recruits on a particularly bad day. He apologised for the shock it had given me and said it helped him wake up in the right spirit and find motivation in the early morning. We needed some to reach the 1800 metres of Telouet.

We left Ouarzazate in good time under the illusion that finally the winds would give us a break. We veered off the main road and cycled past Ben Hadou, where the large Kasbah attracted buses full of tourists. There was a long climb ahead and once again bad karma brought ghastly headwinds no matter which direction we turned. We left the tourists behind and continued up the dramatic valley. The handful of villages we passed by seemed abandoned were it not for the few children playing outside.

Thami El Glaoui, known as   Lord of the Atlas and Pasha of Marrakesh between 1912 and 1956, was born here. During his time he had made this valley the main access point between the desert and the coast. Telouet thrived, but after the fall from favour of the Pasha, a new road was built to the west and these villages were left stranded and a pale shadow of their former glory. They were still charming, the earthy colours of their houses merging with the dry landscape all around. Green patches of the few oases stood out in stark contrast. Winds were gusty, making an already hard day even harder. Far in the distance on the deserted road, I noticed a dark hooded figure approaching. I whispered to Menno that maybe death was calling, putting an end to our tribulations. It wasn't our time, the black clad figure turned out to be a friendly villager taking a stroll on a traditional djellaba.

It was getting too late to reach Telouet. Just before it got dark, with ten miles left to go, we spotted a wrecked Ford van parked by the side of the road. We talked to the owner and agreed an improvised fare. Our bikes were loaded on the back and out of nowhere a few other passengers trickled in and filled all seats. We had just sponsored an improvised Telouet bus service.

- Ait Benhaddou, MOROCCO -

The vehicle looked a bit of a relic and had certainly seen better days. With a lot of trust we all wobbled up the road reaching the little town. Menno and I agreed that with two days of constant head winds we had more than earned the right to cheat. The final day only four hundred metres of altitude separated us from the summit of Tizi 'n Tichka. The wind picked up once more with force just before reaching the top. With a smile on my face I coped with the last few steep bends. Marrakesh was getting nearer and nearer, its distance punctuated by red painted stones along the road. I had one last Japanese sticker left to give. It was all pink and flowers, definitely meant for the ladies. A little girl waved her arms calling me. She welcomed me to her dusty village with her big dark eyes full of joy and hope. I begged that she wouldn't ask for a pen. She was too shy to tell me her name but her smile at receiving the simple gift was something to behold. Finally I had found someone who appreciated my stickers. Her father, standing a little further back, thanked me, yet I had received so much more.

All these friendly and welcoming people had made Morocco a wonderful place to discover. Marrakech was now all the way downhill. We cut right through the city, getting lost and zigzagging our bikes through a maze of souks.

* * *

BACK TO THE COAST

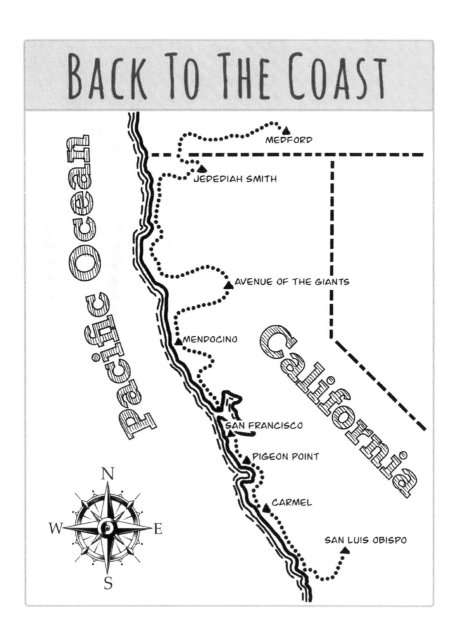

Pacific Ocean

California

MEDFORD

JEDEDIAH SMITH

AVENUE OF THE GIANTS

MENDOCINO

SAN FRANCISCO

PIGEON POINT

CARMEL

SAN LUIS OBISPO

N
W   E
S

Back To The Coast

My first journey down the Pacific Coast had left a mark; when it was time to choose my next destination all I wanted was to experience those same roads one more time. I would have another chance to see places that the fog had kept hidden and see once more those that had most astounded me. Bronte and I would rejoin the cycling caravan, this time starting from the northern border of California and heading south to Los Angeles. After a long flight I was back in San Francisco, where I enjoyed a couple of sightseeing days before a bus journey to Grant Pass, just across the Oregon border.

Fort Mason hostel was a familiar place to stay, with its inspiring location overlooking San Francisco bay. Awful experiences trying to get some sleep in hostels had become part of what being on a holiday meant to me. Years back, while staying in a dorm room here, a snoring competition had escalated into screaming and abuse, one of the contestants threatening to call the police if the growling didn't come to a complete stop. Staying in the large co-ed dorm of about twenty or so bunk beds, I knew I was in for a treat. Indeed rants and growls built up into a symphony that made any effort to sleep vain.

The following day I joined a hostel guided walking tour of the hills of San Francisco, five hours of it. Henry, the elderly but extremely fit volunteer running it, presented himself in good time on the steps of Fort Mason. He introduced himself and gave a prep talk about the tour. He talked of the risks of fatigue and heat stroke and recommended we should carry large quantities of water. All participants set off following his speedy steps like foot soldiers about to attempt a crossing of the Gobi desert. The campaign turned out to be energetic but full of interesting information and hidden gems that only a local would know.

He was very passionate, adding interesting facts and stories that made us forget our aching limbs.

It was time to face the appalling reputation of Greyhound buses and get to the starting point of Grant Pass, Oregon. The historic company offered the cheapest transfers and a well connected network of services but its reputation was marred by reports of violence and a general sense that boarding its buses was done at one's own risk. Not owning a car in the States is a sign of utter failure. The vast majority of passengers relying on buses for their journeys, were those living at the margin of society and a few hapless tourists.

I had heard rumours that Greyhound was also frequently used by ex convicts exiting prison. Apparently, as part of their freedom package, they were issued a free bus ticket too. Worse, there were hints that these buses were also used to transfer current convicts from one minimum security prison to another. California, with its large penitentiaries scattered all over the State, was filling buses with ease.

The network timetables, were the result of a combined effort striving for maximum danger and inconvenience. My bus would leave San Francisco in the evening and reach Sacramento before midnight, where I had to wait for a connecting bus departing at 2:45 am. Hardly any sensible person would contemplate taking a bus with a three hours wait in the middle of the night but I had no choice.

Sacramento station waiting room, by the time I arrived, looked like a busy mental asylum ward. It was packed with drug addicts, alcoholics, convicts and a handful of well intentioned people too. My journey companions turned out to be a distilled version of that unruly lot. While taking my seat I stared at the procession of boarding passengers with increasing concern; I was afraid. There was a man the size of a wardrobe, wobbling to his seat clad in a brown bathrobe towel as a coat, followed by a fidgety man displaying some kind of substance withdrawal symptoms. Next were an intoxicated Spike Lee look-alike, a man immersed in a profound conversation with himself and three unaccompanied dogs. We set off in the early hours of the morning, a mental institution on wheels.

One of the few sensible looking characters was a man in his sixties. He wore an elegant suit and I thought he was rather over dressed for the occasion. In Medford he redeemed himself. As we stopped for a short break to get some food and drinks I sat down at a restaurant table by the window. I glanced outside and there he was, in the centre of the large floodlit parking lot, passionately dancing with himself on an improvised tarmac stage. Entranced, he had to be snapped out of his improvised performance by our strict driver, threatening to depart. Talking of our driver, after years of abuse he was a bit patronising and each time a new passenger got on board he would get on the loudspeaker to issue a long list of reminders and warnings.

"Do not smoke within twenty yards of the bus..."

"Smoke only once you reach a designated area..."

"The conductor is here to assist you but do not distract him while he is driving..."

"If someone is late returning, I will not wait..."

"Do not keep your mobile phones switched on as this might disturb your neighbours..."

"Use earphones with your volume turned down when listening to music..."

"When you reach your stop be careful crossing the road..."

A long list of do's and don'ts. All sensible stuff to my ears but a little too much health and safety for the rowdy lot sitting at the rear.

Rules and more rules that probably reminded them of prison. One could sense their increasing discomfort, the moaning turned louder as the journey progressed and the announcements multiplied. One of them, having reached his destination, cursed abuse while walking out, stepped in front of the bus and ceremoniously raised his middle finger to the driver. A roar of applause erupted from the back rows. We set off for another leg of the journey, now with an upset driver too. We reached Grants Pass, my final destination; Greyhound had spared me and I was relieved that I didn't have to put my life at risk all the way to Vancouver, Canada.

Bronte was reassembled and started spinning the sixty kilometres to Cave Junction Lone Mountain campsite. Jim, the camp host, recommended a blissful dip in the river pond, a few meters away from my tent. Next was Jedediah Smith campsite and its life threatening wildlife: I was looking forward to once again being scared for the night.

- *Jedediah Smith N.P. California, USA* -

Roads were quieter than expected and so was the campsite. Just as I prepared for a lonely night at the hiker biker site, James turned up.

He was one of those unlikely cyclists you meet on the West coast, not so keen on bicycles per se but somehow forced to pedal as a result of the vicissitudes of life. You recognise them by simply asking where they left from and where they are heading to. Free like leaves tossed by the wind, they turn silent, without the slightest concern or clue. James was in his sixties, a most charming man. He had a military discipline and was keen on challenges. His latest one involved a self-imposed ban on tents, relying on a plain tarp and a sleeping bag instead. As grim as it sounded to me, he was full of enthusiasm in his endeavour, reporting how he had successfully endured the harshest conditions in Colorado's sub zero temperatures. His austerity was also a response to a deep and ingrained mistrust of California.

"It's a beautiful State but it is full of thieves." he sanctioned.

"If you are not careful and watch out, you end up stripped down to your pants."

"Damn!" he continued in a complaining tone.
"Each time I come around here, my gear gets lighter and lighter, raided by professional conmen. When I have nothing left I know it is time to turn my bike around and head back home to Virginia."

The evening by the idyllic hiker biker's towering trees, was not as spooky this year, enlivened by a private wedding party in the picnic area by the river, with plenty of music and food. There was no need for any loud radio, the air filled with the warm sounds of a three man bluegrass band instead.

A day later, I was once again cycling along beloved Newton Drury Lane, riding at the feet of massive trees. I reached Elk Prairie and was back on track, joining the southbound traveling pack. Half a dozen cyclists had already pitched their tents and more trickled in as the evening went on.

Jack and his stories were thoroughly missed this year. The centre of attention was a New Jersey girl instead; she had left home with her little dog in May and after four months on the road, she had reached the Pacific coast. The dog traveled in a comfortable basket set at the top of the rear rack and by now had got used to his camping routine. Once it got dark he left us, peacefully walking into his tent, for a well deserved night's rest. Bronte's ability to quickly fold up into a tiny bundle would be put to great use the following day, as I had planned a hundred kilometres cheating transfer on a local bus from Trinidad to Scotia, back to the gates of Avenue of the Giants.

In the morning I was faced with an unexpected challenge in the shape of a grumpy elk. These gently looking but impressive animals are in fact rather unpredictable. Some later research revealed that it is all the fault of Parelaphostrongylus tenuis, a brain-worm that lays eggs in their central nervous system, wreaking havoc with their brain. Severe symptoms include extreme weakness, lameness, walking in circles, partial or complete blindness, loss of fear for humans and mortality. My elk nicely fell into the fearless, uncaring type; her attitude was compounded by her little calves nearby. The imposing animal crossed the little road right in front of me as I was about to exit the campsite. I stopped, faking my best well meaning look. She smelt fear instead and turned around giving me more fearless stares. In my cycling experience I had gained some knowledge of how to deal with dogs or bears, but elk? What is one supposed to do with an elk? Should I sprint and risk being chased or stand still and risk being charged at?

As I was contemplating misery and the menace stood still, growing grumpier by the minute, a good samaritan appeared. A lady had witnessed the impasse; she pulled down the side window of her van and shouted that I had better let her get between us. I happily moved to the other side, let her slide between man and elk and ducked behind,

- Elk Prairie, California, USA -

following her slowly towards the exit. Pride had taken quite a beating but the old self was at least intact and safe. Once in Trinidad, Bronte was quickly folded and packed, I boarded the bus and was whisked past the uninspiring stretches between Arcata and Eureka. In a couple of hours I was delivered a few pedal strokes from the entrance of Avenue of the Giants.

I reached the visitor centre and Burlington Camp, where I regretted not having been able to stop in the past. Pitching my tent in the hiker biker site I met Gerritt, a Dutch man who was cycling on a recumbent bike from Alaska to Mexico, and Spencer, a Canadian from Edmonton on his way to Ecuador or so. We all enjoyed a good evening chat and shared our cycling plans. Avenue of the Giants was not less stunning the second time around. The going was slow as every corner demanded me to stop, admire the views and record pictures and videos that always failed to replicate the emotions I felt. I would share them on and off all day with Gerritt and Spencer as we repeatedly bumped into each other and shared sights that filled us with inspiration and awe.

A few hours later I was back in Garberville, welcomed by a Slovenian guy I had met on the bus the previous day. He had been traveling with a blind man. I asked whether he was a friend and was told an interesting story. He had been a couple of days with no money due to some issues with his bank. In Eureka he then met this man who wanted to go to Garberville but needed help with directions as he was blind. He also told him he had terminal cancer. Helping the man he was offered food and motel costs but mostly, as he said, the experience made his difficult situation of having to cope without money irrelevant and easy to bear. Gerritt introduced me to a couple of guys from Quebec. Young and naive in their enthusiasm, they had left home with light, frail racing bikes that were most unsuitable for carrying the weight of their bags. Their days were punctuated by visits to all the bike shops they could find along the way, trying to patch up an ever increasing number of failures and breakdowns.

Regularly smoking during the day and at the campsite, their lungs were in tatters. One could hear their presence by the loud wheezing and coughing coming up the road. In Standish Hickey, their progress hampered by mechanical and health issues, it suddenly dawned on them that they were seriously behind schedule. They emerged from their smokey tent in a panic, asking us whether they would be able to reach San Francisco in three days, making it on time for their flight home. A lost cause indeed. They were never to be seen again on the road, leaving us hoping that a gentle soul had been kind enough to offer them some rescue. Leggett Hill was climbed with some trepidation. I was wary of the foggy days I had experienced in the past, but this time there were just a few patches that very soon cleared.

The internet has brought wonders to our lives but after two decades it had also turned people into addicts. Campsites usually didn't offer any connection and we were left to deal with our withdrawal symptoms. Come the morning, we were all pretending to be cycling down the coast while in fact we were desperately searching for some signal on our phones. Having left Gerritt behind, Spencer and I reached our next campsite as a mauve sun disappeared beyond the ocean line. At about seven o'clock, just as we had given up the idea of seeing him, flashing lights pierced the night. His recumbent bike whizzed down the steep descent, a grin and a sigh of relief painted on his face. I rode together with Spencer for a few more days as foggy patches came and went, offering a pleasant relief from the baking sun. As far as Gerritt was concerned, Alaska was taking its toll, and tiredness had caught up with him and stopped him short. His recumbent bike with waving flags never reappeared, and I wished I had at least had the time to say goodbye.

After walking the hills of San Francisco with Henry, it was time to cycle some with Bronte. As I was about to reach the top of La Honda I got a taste of fear. One of the most popular biking and cycling roads in the Bay Area, it winds up Skyline twisty and narrow, connecting Silicon Valley to the ocean. Being so popular with local cyclists made me think it would be relatively safe; it turned out to be anything but. Hordes of software engineers, IT millionaires and young entrepreneurs were testing their latest Ferraris, Porsches and monster bikes and this was their weekend race track. As I was slowly cycling my way up around a tight bend, I heard a screeching of brakes and tires right behind me; next I felt myself gently pushed up and off the side of road.

A lady emerged from the car in tears.

"Oh my god! Are you alright? I am so sorry..." she screamed with a shaky voice.

The wisest words I came up with were "Go slow for f**k sake."

"I mean, I could have killed you...!" she said, as if I needed reminding.

Luckily unhurt my attention was all for Bronte, who surely I thought must have been damaged in some way. The back wheel was not moving freely and the rack was bent.

"Are you sure you are ok? I mean...can I give you a lift somewhere?" she continued, by now a total wreck on the verge of a breakdown.

Given her state and driving skills I thought it best to refuse.

"No thanks. Hopefully you've learnt something today and will be more careful next time." said the wise in me, regaining some composure.

"Oh you are so nice." she sobbed.

"Well I am still alive, there's still something to be positive about."

I walked the remaining distance to the top where the weekend racers were celebrating their mad speed in the sunshine. One of them helped me to straighten my rack. The bike had taken a hit but seemed miraculously fine. Wary of some hidden damage and more bad driving I slowly dived down the other side heading for the coast. Heavy Sunday traffic followed me down the Cabrillo Highway into Half Moon Bay where it was time to get acquainted with new friends. There was Gina from Australia, and also Amy and Victor, a couple of cyclists from Colorado. After pitching what looked like a ten man tent, the two of them began their daily ritual. A wine bottle was uncorked and savoured in style in two elegant traveling plastic flutes. They were wandering cyclists, bicycle lovers, married - not surprisingly - while riding a bike through a chapel in Vegas.

The hills were now gentler, a strong tail wind pushed me past Pigeon Point, a quaint lighthouse now transformed into a hostel. Quite an amazing spot it was, it left me wishing I could stay for the night. There were to be navigational issues in Santa Cruz, where not getting lost proved quite a challenge.

- Pigeon Point, California, USA -

It took the fellowship of riders quite a while to figure out the way to the next campsite. Perched on top of steep cliffs I could jot down notes in my diary, overlooking seagulls and dolphins playing with the wind and the waves. The youngest cyclists ever joined us that night too: Jack and John, two years old twins, pulled down the coast on board a trailer by their adventurous if slightly reckless parents.

I had planned taking a shuttle ride to Monterey but in the end realised I still had time to spare and decided to ride on instead. Victor had recommended I stop short of Los Angeles, where traffic was too heavy to enjoy the ride.

San Luis Obispo would be my final destination. I briefly turned inland in the outskirts of the Central Valley where interminable farms extended as far as the eye could see. Mexican labourers were picking strawberries, scattered tiny dots bent down in the sweltering heat. I felt a little uneasy. I was enjoying some of my finest hours while these poor souls had to endure back-breaking days for some spare change. Monterey was not the forlorn little town of Steinbeck's Cannery Row anymore. It seemed to have it all, blessed with prosperity, stable sun, oysters and good wines. I couldn't afford its prices and I wasn't alone it seemed.

All the 'have nots' ended up spending a most interesting night at the Monterey Veterans Memorial Park. California's good weather, take it easy-life and hippy styles, are a magnet for vagrants and travellers. Compared to the local Hiltons and Marriotts, Veterans Memorial, at six dollars a night, was a steal. Excluding Jeff, Scott, the trailing twins and other bikers I had recently met, the rest of the campsite population consisted mostly of bums. I returned late from an evening downtown; the twins were taking it in turn to scream and cry, probably scared by their destitute neighbours. This set off a Monterrey County dogs and wolves howling contest. A lady, frustrated by a proficient snorer, decided in the middle of the night to relocate tent and daughter to a quieter spot, dispensing curses in the process. As far as my direct neighbour goes, I had plenty of complaints. Until about midnight he held the most interesting of conversations. No eavesdropping was involved, he was loud enough to be heard loud and clear despite the radio blasting news through my earphones.

His real name was Howard, a popular chap whose mobile phone seemed busier than a call centre in Mumbai. On dating sites he was known as Steve, divorced with three kids, a girl 17, and two boys 20 and 21. He held an hour long conversation with Monica who lived in Pacifica. She had the great misfortune to stumble on his profile and was by now probably wondering whether she had finally met the guy of her life. Howard..., sorry Steve, was a very smooth talker. He told her how he was a stage actor by profession and a host to popular radio shows in LA.

"I recently bought a house in Monterey." he said.

Quite a story given the fact that he was stuck in a tent instead. The most disturbing news came later in another conversations with a female friend of his.

It went something like this:

"You know I am a strong man and always get through challenges, don't you?"

"How do you think I survived years in jail, sharing my cell with those murderers."

This was not the kind of information I was eager to hear in the middle of the night from a nearby tent.

- Carmel, California, USA -

The following morning, campers mood was pretty low, with widespread migraines and a general lack of goodwill. As far as us cyclists were concerned, we all had a common goal. Get ready and ride as fast as we could down that hill. After sharing a night with convicts, Seventeen Mile ride, Pacific Grove, Pebble Beach and Carmel seemed a world apart. I was able to witness the incredible spectacle of several humpback whales feeding on sardines, their arching silhouettes emerging and diving just a stone's throw away from the beach. I reached Pfeiffer Sur State Park, a stark contrast from Veterans Memorial and one of the best campgrounds I had visited so far. The hiker biker itself was set on a shaded, quiet corner. It was reached crossing a wooden bridge over a brook and set in the midst of a spacious redwood grove. Jeff from San Diego was there, his cigarette lit, celebrating with smoke the end of another long day.

At night I was woken up by the sound of rain ticking on my tent. By early morning, I was left with no choice but to start my day facing the damp. A bit of a shock after the pleasant weather enjoyed continuously for a couple of weeks. Heavy fog piled on the misery. It prevented any meaningful views. but my main concern was not being run over by cars on this twisty and narrow road. It was midday, but so dark that it felt like midnight. I slowly descended the mountain facing the storm, praying that my red rear lights would keep flashing.

Approaching Gorda and descending to San Simeon the sky finally opened, light returned, uncovering a timid sun that was just enough to allow me to dry. I stopped at the sea lions beach, which I remembered visiting many years before and was much more crowded this time around. Having reached San Simeon State Park, James and I began the unpleasant task of unfolding and pitching our soaked wet tents.

Now only a few miles of cycling separated me from San Luis Obispo. Cycling along Turri Road, pushed by a strong tail wind, it didn't take that long to reach the finish line and freeze the instant in a final picture with James. San Luis Obispo was still the prosperous university town I remembered. Top of the agenda was a return to Firestone, where I was able once again to taste their memorable Pig Sandwich.

- San Luis Obispo, California, USA -

MANGOES AND CURRIES

Thailand

Mangoes and Curries

My unrelenting effort to manipulate the weather and cycle back into summer led me next to Thailand. I left the darkness of a winter morning wrapped up in layers of clothing and was delivered into blinding sunshine. It wasn't quite Thailand yet, but almost. A quick stopover in Malaysia for a day was necessary, so I joined the connecting crowds that use Kuala Lumpur airport in order to get somewhere else.

Often abbreviated to KL as if it were an airline code, it seemed a sought after destination to nurse hangovers and strong jet lags. I don't want to seem too unkind. It is a thriving capital populated by extremely welcoming people. Malaysia has much to offer, but pretty much anything is elsewhere and far from the city. KL hasn't decided yet what it wants to be, and out of this inferiority complex it is trying to compete by means of tall towers and skyscrapers. It suited me and the many sleepy tourists in search of interesting sites. Most seemed satisfied to at least get a selfie in front of a red sculpted 'I love KL', not quite knowing why.

The following day I was in for a choppy start in Thailand. My bad luck began with the flight being delayed, and continued once arrived at Chiang Mai airport. A particularly stroppy immigration officer was not having the best of days. I had done all my homework and filled in and signed my entry form before joining the long queue. Having reached the boot, ready for judgement, I was asked the impossible question.

"Where staying tonight?"

The officer pointed to a line that had been left empty, not out of negligence but simply because I didn't have a clue. If the worst came to the worst I was carrying a tent.

His stern look demanded an explanation.

"You see, I am cycling and as I am not sure how far I will be able to go, I will look for a place along the way".

It was the wrong answer, and I could tell by the change of tone in his voice.

"I can't let you through if you don't know where you stay. Go to that gate over there and they will help you."

I joined a group of rejected 'farang', a word often heard, approximately meaning 'bloody foreigners'. Even in a land of gentle souls like Thailand, a uniform and some authority is all it takes to get a potential jerk. The officer we were referred to was not in a better mood and certainly not willing to help. I overheard the person in front of me saying he wasn't sure where he was staying for the night. Making matters worse, he started arguing and getting upset, probably the last thing one should do. The stroppy officer exited his boot and, throwing a tantrum, told him to sit down and wait. Nobody knew for what.
"Next!", he shouted, giving me quite a look.

I knew my chances were slim. I started explaining that I also wasn't sure where I would be spending the night, at which point he heaved a sigh in total despair. Sagging back in his chair he covered his face with both hands, pondering what was wrong with life. By now it was quite clear that writing down the Ritz, Place Vendome, Paris would have probably been good enough. The bloody foreigners were once more rejected and had to search for a better plan. Mobile phones were switched on and fingers started typing in search for the cheapest place to book online.

We all settled for the identical place. Some enterprising soul, aware of this bureaucratic hurdle, was advertising two dollar rooms in central Chiang Mai. They probably didn't exist, but were perfect for people stuck at the airport who would never turn up and stay.

One by one we produced our fake hotel address and reservation numbers. Reluctantly he gave in and let us all through. With all these delays I had to break my record for unpacking the bike and was soon ready to make the most of the dwindling daylight. Unlike KL, where everybody's English was better than mine, here the further away from the city I moved the less I was understood. Road signs turned full Thai as I cycled on, missing all the right turns. In my lack of preparation I didn't even know what the Thai words for hotel or guest house looked or sounded like. As it turned darker I had to rely on some gentle souls to draw me a detailed map showing me where one could be found.

I was on my first full day on the bike, at the start of the Mae Hong Son loop, a popular roller coaster up and down Thailand's highest mountains. An old favourite amongst motorists and riders, it skims the Burmese border and in about nine days it should have brought me back to Chiang Mai. Moving further away from the city onto small rural roads, the cycling turned more relaxing and enjoyable. Short tempered officers had given way to gentle Thais, who never failed to ask me where I had left my wife. I visited a tiger sanctuary but resisted the temptation to get too close. Here, imposing and powerful predators raised in captivity were so domesticated that for enough Baht you could even hug them. I watched the odd spectacle of tourists taking selfies while 'courageously' patting their belly or holding a tail in their hands. They seemed well looked after, but I felt a little sorry for the tigers' fate. Maybe they didn't mind having to put up with countless photographs with strangers. I was told by one of the rangers that each one of them got fed one hundred kilograms of meat each day. Should that not be delivered on time I suppose there were always a couple of easy preys up for grabs.

- Huai Pha, THAILAND -

Talking of food, countryside roads were like an open kitchen. I couldn't help but feel peckish and it was hard to cycle past sizzling Pad Thais and delicious curries unperturbed. As the road started climbing with ridiculous grades I had to take my first few walks. Lots of stray dogs reminded me of Sri Lanka. Were it not for the experience gained there, I am sure some would have happily set off on a chase. The fiercest dogs seemed to roam around temples. I wondered whether they ended up there to work through some past bad karma. Monks who vowed peace and harmlessness were surely well protected by all that barking.

On my first night in a mountain village, having found a place to stay, I started searching for some food. English was useless around here. As a way to find out whether there was a restaurant nearby, I walked towards an elderly couple sitting on their veranda and pointed at my mouth. I was asked to sit down at a table while the wife started chopping ingredients and cooking up an improvised dish of chicken, eggs and rice. When I asked how much it was they looked at each other, not quite knowing. They scribbled a sixty on a piece of paper, short of a couple of dollars for a delicious meal. Whether it was a restaurant or their home I will never know.

Language was always quite a barrier, but luckily this cycling business was simple. All I needed to be able to survive were a handful of foreign sounds. Like a trained parrot I strived to learn some badly pronounced basics like 'hello', 'thank you', 'water', 'hotel' and 'food'. In order to understand road signs I needed some reading skills too. All efforts in this direction ended in total failure. It was interesting to see how my brain worked. Being completely unfamiliar with the way to write and pronounce each character, it was impossible to recognize words. All I could see were worm-like shapes, sometimes straight and at other times with their tails twirled. The unfortunate association made matters worse because the more I focused on a word the more it seemed to come to life and wiggle. I gave up pretty soon. It was bad enough trying to make sense of them while they stood still, let alone when they were moving.

Most mornings I was rising above foggy mountains with the unusual experience of feeling cold in Thailand. Thai people left their homes as if they were about to face a Canadian winter. In fresh but pleasant temperatures they walked about in woolly hats, scarves and down jackets, and still shivered. I briefly met Carter, a young guy from Seattle who was cycling around the same way with an age advantage of a few decades. He asked me whether I fancied a race. If at all possible I wanted to go even slower. Climbing further into the mountains the endless food stalls of the planes disappeared and I had to overdose on multivitamins to make it to the top.

Eager to fill up my empty stomach I dropped down into Pai, a town on the hippy trail and, according to most guidebooks, the place to go partying in the mountains. Young farangs had moved in and conquered it, far outnumbering locals. Wearing colourful clothes they would never have dared wear back home, they walked barefoot in their baggy trousers, with long hair and beards à la Jesus Christ. After a breakfast that lasted hours, I was happy to evacuate sleepy Pai and return to Thailand.

I timed my departure to coincide with the rural newspaper despatch service. The pickup van drove slowly along the emergency lane of the road with stereo loudspeakers blasting the news of its imminent arrival. Every now and then people would scramble out of the thickets in order to make a purchase. Because of the frequent stops and the fact that he was driving slowly to not miss his sales we were never too far. The speaker system ran an automated loop that, no matter how much I hated it, I learnt off by heart within about half an hour.

It went something like this:

"Wan chisan hey! mat kara kom chun wat chisan boom cha chan chiiiii!!!!" Great emphasis on the ending here.
"Ran nan na chain pro bri bri pro dreng dreeeeng!"

The pickup was running on an old diesel engine that had the carbon footprint of a jet plane. Each time it started moving when I was close by I disappeared in a puff of black smoke. Sometimes I would be able to overtake, wishing the driver a flat tyre, but before too long he would catch up and I could hear the loop re-emerging. It made me cycle faster than I had to. The drill sounded more like the voice of a Sergeant Major wanting to pick a fight with his new recruits than a sales pitch. Carter caught up with me halfway up the mountain, never to be seen again. He was definitely winning the race.

Whoever planned and built these mountain roads would have benefited greatly from a visit to Switzerland or Austria to see how it is properly done. In the valleys you had these meandering roads full of twists and turns, then as soon as the climb started it was up a straight ramp. Watching cars, I wondered whether they might somersault and come right back down. As for me, when I had to brake uphill in order not to lose ground, I knew it was time for a walk.

In the village of Soppong I had to give in and admit defeat to a stomach bug that saw me spend the best part of three days and nights on a toilet seat. Thailand, I must admit, had a history of messing up my digestive system. A decade before I had a rather humiliating episode following an inspiring cookery class held by a Thai celebrity chef. We were taken out to his countryside pad where he introduced us to the wonderful scent of local spices and ingredients before showing us how to cook a full meal. Each of the participants was later given the opportunity to replicate each dish and then feast on his own finished menu. Perhaps my cooking skills left something to be desired, but, at the end of the day, while traveling back to Chiang Mai, things got so bad that I considered jumping out of a speeding taxi. Only shear determination and some yogic breathing techniques allowed me to reach my hotel entrance gates with some sense of dignity and respect. I managed to pay the fare before sprinting towards the outdoor swimming pool area without saying a thank you or a goodbye. A cleaning lady was mopping the floor of the only available toilet but there were no language barriers then. I stormed the place with some loud cursing and grand gestures, evicted the intruder and just about managed to lock the door behind me. I hope she has since forgiven me.

Let's be positive and say that Soppong - or Pang Mapha, according to whom you asked - was the perfect place to heal a bad stomach. The lively village was lacking any points of interest beyond the outdoor market. Usually at least a little temple rescues the most forlorn of places in Thailand, but the local one, a short walk up the hill, was a rather gloomy building topped by a roof made of asbestos. The only reason why tourists stopped in Soppong was to take part in group treks of its intricate mountain caves.

- Mae Hong Son, THAILAND -

I couldn't think of anything worse than being stuck deep down in the confined spaces of a cave with diarrhoea in the company of a bunch of strangers and a guide. The best I could do was reserve a comfortable room. Without any distractions I could focus on well timed toilet runs. I had a caring landlady with an endless supply of toilet paper, a pharmacy not too far away and, should things go really south, a little hospital too. A most kind pharmacist welcomed me every morning with the traditional Thai greeting. His hands folded and with a slight bow, he uttered the ritual 'sawadikap' before delving into the intricacies of my bowel movements. At each visit the quantity of sachets and tablets increased. Eventually he decided to go nuclear, prescribing some antibiotics which did the trick. By the third day I finally got back the will to live and was very pleased with the quality of my stools.

The high season well over, the landlady had got used to a reliable income from my room and must have been sad to see me leaving. I was back on the roads of north west Thailand with a grin. Of course a little weakened and dehydrated, but glad to be operating my bike gears rather than a flush handle. I deserved the atmospheric early morning ride. A low fog wrapped the valley, every now and then uncovering steep hills and patches of blue sky behind. I crossed paths with a Dutch couple, who were seven months into a round-the-world bike trip, before meeting Andy, a Swiss professional triathlete who was training here. He overtook me several times on his light, carbon racing bike.

I reached Mae Hong Son, a surprisingly beautiful mountain town with impressive Shan temples scattered around a small lake. While walking to the monastery up the hill just in time for sunset and the best view in town, Andy once again ran past me. He was now on the running part of his daily training. He waved at me and said that after 180 kilometres of cycling he was ending the day with several sprints up and down the hill. The following day at sunrise I was once again cycling up to Doi Kongmu temple, hoping to catch some views with the morning fog. As expected, the fog was there, so much so that it shrouded the entire landscape. Bad luck. Speaking to a couple of Thai tourists, I heard that the day before at the same time, the fog had lowered down the valley and the view was stunning.

It was getting unbearably hot and humid. Despite daily showers and frequent rinsing of clothes, by eleven in the morning I was mouldy. I briefly moved away from the mountains to rolling hills and rice fields but this Mae Hong Son loop was not for the faint hearted. What I thought should be an easy stretch without too much climbing ended up being a constant up and down steep hills with legs aching.

A signpost I spotted along the way reminded me why I was here. In large bold red letters it read "Mae Hon Song 1864 curves, Thailand". I had long lost count of how many I had passed so far but I knew I was well over half way. On top of a hill with a terrace vista, I spotted a four-wheel drive car nervously parking.

An elegant caucasian lady wearing a colourful sarong dismounted and began scanning the place, with panicky looks at me and at the fields down below. She then started a brisk walk, disappearing in the wilderness, nowhere to be seen. A few minutes later I spotted her naked bum re-emerging from the thick grasses as she struggled to pull up her clothes. She had all my sympathy. I was reassured to know that bad stomachs were not a prerogative of scruffy cyclists.

Thick fogs were my constant companion along this ride. In the early hours of the morning I was repeatedly moving in and out of misty clouds. Little droplets stuck to my face and clothes keeping me fresh for at least half of the morning. People were always most friendly and at every interaction I only wished I could speak some Thai. Off the beaten track English was not spoken and the only communication I could have was via some improvised sign language and a lot of laughter. It was still some way to Mae Sariang, a hundred kilometres of steep hills continuously breaking my pace. At times I wished I could be back climbing roads in the Indian Himalayas. There, I could focus on going up all day, felt rewarded for the gained altitude and adjust to a comfortable speed I could keep all day. Here, a stream of motorbikes overtaking offered regular encouragement. Despite years of farang cyclists pedalling up and down these roads, they probably didn't make sense of me and wondered why I hadn't hired a cheap motorbike instead. On the seventh day on the Mae Hong Son route I was saved like an Adventist. Not by Jesus' second coming but rather by a group of Buddhist monks eager to build up a credit of good karma. A twist of events whisked me two hundred kilometres away, back to charming Chiang Mai. Before we jump ahead let me explain how it all happened.

After yet another gruelling day of a 'duathlon' with lots of walks interrupted by brief spells of cycling, this was turning more and more into an initiation rite rather than adventure biking. I held on, climbing over two thousand metres for the first time, but as the incessant slog continued, dark thoughts started creeping in.

They said mostly uncaring things like:

"Come on, after two days of dysentery, you deserve better…"

"You are two days late! What about the rest of the ride around Chiang Rai?"

"You idiot! Why didn't you board that bus you saw in Mae Sariang…"

As the light of the day was dimming I reached Wat Kiew Lom, a little mountain village and my final destination for the day. According to cycling wisdom researched on the internet this was the only place around where I would be able to find a room for rent. The tiny village was obviously in the midst of a grand wedding or some kind of major party. I was only half surprised to hear that the few beds available were taken. With hardly thirty minutes of daylight left and fading energies there was nowhere else I could go to. I started walking towards the local temple, resigned to spending a night of prayers on hard wooden benches when the 'Buddha van' came to my rescue. I noticed a classic red taxi van carrying monks approaching. It was obviously taken but in a desperate attempt I still shouted for some attention. The unwavering driver shook his head in clear disapproval so all my hopes rested on the monks. They must have thought it was the perfect chance to collect a good deed because the taxi suddenly U-turned and came back stopping by my side.

"Where are you going?" asked one of the monks.

"Wherever you go is fine…" I said imagining it would surely involve being able to have a meal and a roof over my head for the night.
"I explained the sad turn of events and looking at the map I pointed at Hot, a town a few hours down the valley.

"We go there, you can join us."

- Chiang Mai, THAILAND -

I shifted my folded bike and gear between potted plants and plastic boxes and sat on the bench next to three monks. It got even better. As we approached the town down the other side of the mountain I pointed at the map wondering to which monastery they were going. The only monk that could speak some broken English uttered the magical word.

"We go Chiang Mai." Bingo!

A few hours later they dropped me off a few kilometres from the city centre, far away from hard wooden benches. After a couple of days admiring the wonderful temples and alleys of Chiang Mai, at 7:59 I was ready for the bus transfer to Chiang Rai. As I was packing my bike at the strike of the hour the national anthem blasted out from a series of loudspeakers. Everyone stopped what they were doing; people who were seated waiting for their bus stood up and started chanting. I had no clue as to what was going on but out of respect I also stood still and stopped packing. I later realised it was the custom of a proud nation and a regular 8 am event around the country. The previous days I had noticed the early morning chanting in the schoolyards as well as kids energetically sweeping and cleaning the front yard. I must say it was quite impressive.

Another wonderful Thai tradition I witnessed most days was monks going on their alms round. Entire families waited patiently in front of their doors with fresh food and other donations ready. Other times it was the monks that stood waiting for someone to come. Either way both got their rewards. Lay people started the day with a generous gift and monks were reminded that without this support they wouldn't be able to live the life they lived.

After the Mae Hong Son ramps training and a little rest for sightseeing in Chiang Rai, I was ready once again to put my legs of steel to good use. The hundred kilometres to Phayao went as smooth as breeze. After whingeing about the crookedness of Thailand's roads I got my fair share of long straights and roads as flat as pancakes. Sometimes lack of communication helps to save one's face. I stumbled into a procession in the middle of the road. Two leading monks held the end of two thick ropes, followed by a cheerful crowd pulling what seemed, from a distance, like a white chariot. Firecrackers were thrown on the road as people smiled at me asking me to join in. I had hardly asked the policeman whether it was a village party when the chariot passed right in front of me. It was loaded with flowers and a white coffin. The policeman smiled at me. Luckily he had not understood.

My cycling in rural Thailand was about to end with a final stretch between Phayao and Phrae, two very relaxed and interesting little towns. In these country villages there was no wasting time in the mornings. Cockfighting being a national sport in Thailand, lots of cockerels were kept in bell-shaped bamboo cages outside in front yards. By five am they were ready to vent all their frustrations: let it be known that they were pissed off to the limit and ready for a good fight.

- Phrae, THAILAND -

I didn't mind it too much because in order to avoid the heat I was doing most of my cycling in the early hours of the morning. By eleven o'clock the temperature and humidity had risen and made everything so much harder.

After the foggy rides in the mountains I was now riding through hazy skies filled with smoke from forest fires. Clear views of what I am sure would have been a nice landscape were hard to come by. By the end of this journey I had developed an extreme fondness of 7/11 Convenience Stores coffee. Each time I spotted the sign by the side of the road I was moved to the brink of tears. It had something to do with the generous addition of condensed milk, an old Vietnamese trick. I had visited Bangkok ten years before but, all cycling finished, a couple of days visiting the Grand Palace and hopping on and off boats speeding on the klongs seemed the perfect end to another journey.

* * *

CANYONS AND MESAS

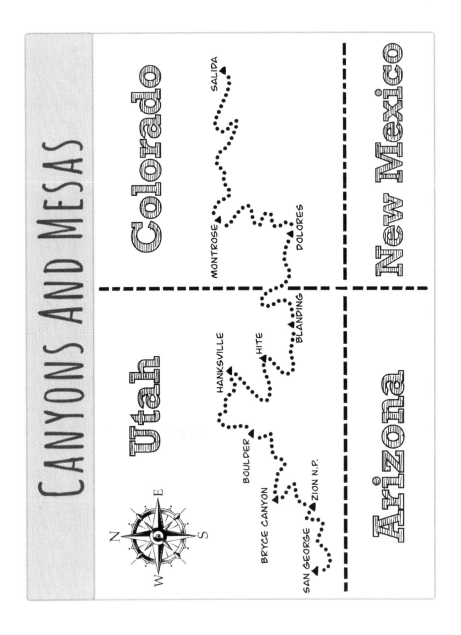

Colorado

New Mexico

SALIDA

MONTROSE

DOLORES

Utah

HANKSVILLE

HITE

BLANDING

BOULDER

BRYCE CANYON

ZION N.P.

SAN GEORGE

Arizona

Canyons and Mesas

I t was nearly the end of May but there were hardly any hints of summer in England. Listening to the radio on the way to the airport, boring news of yet another general election was enlivened by the adventures of the British ambassador to Austria. Mr Turner, more used to being whisked through Hapsburg palaces and elegant receptions, had survived an aggressive wild boar's chase in the woods of Vienna. The excited newsreader recounted how the ambassador was taking a walk on a rainy day when he chanced upon a group of some twenty wild boars. He had to scramble for safety up a pile of wet tree trunks, injuring himself in the process. Needless to say he returned to the embassy in distress and in tatters.

"I had some experience of wild boar." he later said.

"I know that they are mostly shy, and keep out of the way."

"My approach has always been to assume that they are more frightened of me than I am of them." he commented.

In a freak of nature they hadn't shown any signs of fear.

Bronte and I were about to board a plane bound for Las Vegas, ready for a new cycling ramble, this time up and down the mountains of Utah and Colorado. Having arrived in Las Vegas, the shuttle bus from the airport to downtown provided a free introductory tour of this amusement park on steroids. Rising from the bare Mojave desert sands, towers of light and cathedrals of kitsch brightly lit the night sky.

On reaching downtown the night turned into a neon-lit day. Young crowds in their best outfits were seeking joy in the promises of an extraordinary Saturday night out. Competing for attention were live shows by stars such as Elton John, Puff Daddy, Britney Spears, Santana, Celine Dion and Jennifer Lopez. All these showbiz royalties were ready to unleash their talent within little more than a square mile. You could gamble, dance, party, shop or eat to your heart's desire. Everything seemed abundant, nothing was out of reach or out of sight. Even though only a standby cyclist and a passerby, I couldn't help feeling the excitement of this entertainment bribe. Wandering inside the hotels and casinos was an experience in itself. Always vast and grand, they were built around extravagant themes. Caesar's Palace, Venetian, Mirage were some of their evocative names. Of course at the centre of it all was gambling. Ground floors were dedicated entirely to the peculiar addiction of losing one's hard earned cash.

Vegas being just a stepping point for me, I was about to board yet another 'Gravehound' bus to the town of Saint George. Just across the Utah border, the town had been chosen as the starting point: from here the cycling would begin. I have been severe in my reviews of Greyhound in the past. I must admit this time around scheduling had greatly improved and I was able to reserve a sensible 2 pm departure time. Whether this was a good or a bad thing I didn't know. If nothing else, in broad daylight I would at least be able to assess the danger. Having reached Central Station, I started a preliminary passenger scan. Tattoos were in. Grooming very much out. I tried to mess up my tidy hair to look a bit more the part.

Gender equality was definitely improving. Our allocated driver was a Beyonce lookalike with a sergeant major temper and nerves of steel. She had some Guinness record-breaking long nails and eyelashes too. Customer service was still very much left wanting. We were lined up in a military straight line as Beyonce started inspecting our tickets. She gave each of us a stern look and a 'can't be bothered' sigh, before reluctantly letting us board. There was not a smile in sight. The general mood of all the passengers sagged, as if we were at the start of a bus journey to clink. One shouldn't be too quick to judge appearances, but passengers' profiles seemed to confirm that too.

My seat neighbour carried a thick duvet and a large pillow that she tossed and turned in an effort to find the most comfortable position on a dreadful two days journey to Minneapolis. Seated behind me were a guy with two paper clips piercing his ears and his neighbour wearing a red bandana wrapped around his head and a joint skilfully hanging from his pursed lips. They were talking chemistry, expounding on the wonders of Colorado's recently legalised marijuana. They were debating the benefits of 'capsules' and wondering how many cake slices it takes to get stoned. Our commander in chief finally boarded and, standing tall at the front of the bus, started a well rehearsed speech on conduct, putting us firmly through the straight and narrow.

The idea for this trip had been suggested half a year before by my friend Menno. His invitation to join him and Thomas, a friend from Montana, for part of their journey from San Francisco to Colorado, was too hard to resist. I had planned to meet them halfway in Utah but it all went haywire due to accidents, medical emergencies and other curses and delays. They had hardly left San Francisco when Thomas, climbing the third hill, felt poorly and ended up in an operating theatre needing a heart bypass. As for Menno, on top of the delays assisting his friend, the latest news reported further misfortunes. He heard about the death of one of his dogs back in the Netherlands, and a few days later a car crashed into him. It left him with only minor scratches, but triggered a leg infection that needed a few doctor's visits. Hearing such a long chain of misfortunes I wondered if Menno would ever make it.

It was with some apprehension that the third cyclist was about to set off. From Las Vegas I reached the starting point of Saint George and lost one hour in the process as I moved into a different time zone. Bronte, still wrapped up and folded in its bag, was finally allowed to stretch out, displaying all its mechanical wonders. A short cycle away from the bus station were Bob and Carol, a couple of keen cyclists who had offered me free accommodation while in town. They welcomed me with a cocktail, a large burger and wonderful warmth and hospitality. A few years before they had crossed the US in a tandem. They whetted my appetite by telling me that my route would go through the best part of it all. I couldn't wait.

The following morning, Bob led me to the cycle path, making sure that I would find the right way out of town, and waved a final goodbye. A few hours later I was riding along a hot and dry desert road. There was a little traffic every now and then and I met the first few cyclists too. Scott was first. Despite his sleek racing bike he slowed down, riding by my side. I learnt how his mom was originally from Sicily, and he was candid about the fact that her family had some involvement with the local mafia.

"I don't mess around with the 'family' when I go to Sicily." he said.

"When I walk around town they all stare at me and move out of the way." he continued.
"They are all scared. I look too much like them you see. I hate it!"

He was a man bearing some grudges.

Top of his list were Quebecois Canadians.

"You speak English to them and they pretend to not understand. What the hell!"

"Still nothing like Mormons. They make my beer weak." he said.

"All one gets in Utah is 3.2 percent alcohol, can you believe it?"

"Do they drink?" I asked.

- Zion National Park, Utah, USA -

"Oh... they do," he said with a smirk, "only when nobody's watching."

"Anyway, I regularly cross the border into Nevada and get proper beer from there."

Having reached Zion National Park it was soon clear that I would have some trouble finding a place to stay. Hordes had swarmed into Springdale, the village at the heart of the park. A little late I discovered it was Memorial Day weekend, the busiest few days of the year in the park. Campsites rangers had no mercy on cyclists and I had resigned myself to searching for a secluded patch of grass where I could spend the night. I spotted two loaded touring bikes parked outside the library. They belonged to Ross and Jeremy. Much more prepared than I was, they had secured a spot at the main campsite, reserving it well in advance. They kindly offered to share it with me.

The following day I was ready to explore. It was hot, I was still a little jet lagged and tired, but it was going to be one of the best cycling days of my life. Zion National Park is the third most visited park in the United States for a good reason. I had high expectations having visited similar granite wonders in Yosemite, a place I much loved and hoped one day to return to. Mountains here were just as spectacular. Jeremy and Ross, unlike me, were at the end of their journey from Colorado. Having cycled from the opposite direction they gave me some hints on what to expect. They had great news about prevailing winds. For most of their journey I heard how strong winds had hit their face. We are no sailors, but cyclists take a special interest in winds too.

I wanted to beat the crowds and as two deer peacefully grazed the lawn around my tent, I waved goodbye to my cycle buddies. I set off for Zion Canyon Scenic drive. This one lane road was banned to private traffic but it was luckily open for cyclists. The early hours of the morning provided enough peace to take all the spectacle in. The winding road carved its way deep at the bottom of a canyon by the Virgin river, granite mountains towering over on both sides. As an introduction to my journey it couldn't have been more beautiful and inspiring. Having left the drive, a zig zag climb took me further up the mountains. I knew that half way up, a long tunnel was off limits to bikes. The road being narrow, traffic was moving in alternate ways. Cars were queueing for their turn to be granted access. I pedalled on to the front hoping to find a lift.

I succeeded on my first attempt. A party of four friends, going canyoning up the mountains, were more than pleased to let me and my gear sit at the back of their pickup van. We pierced the mountain and I was delivered to the other side. I continued the climb through a stark mountain landscape whose rocks were sometimes marble-white and at other times layered in shades of amber. I had lots of supporters, thumbs-up often stretched out from cars' windows, spurring me on. I imagined being a kind of Tour de France hero, leaving an invisible pack of riders behind. It was hot, and water was never enough. Before running too low, I stopped along the road and asked the camper van lot if they had some to spare. Invariably they had tanks full of it. I received complimentary bottles and countless refills. I was learning some good skills that would be of use once I reached the driest parts of Glen Canyon and Canyonlands National Park. I fast reached a plateau at almost two thousand meters. All prophecies of tail winds came true and pushed me along as if I had a jet engine strapped to my back.

In Utah they frequently used the expression 'holy moly'. It summed up my initial impressions of these first few days. I had hardly left one stunning National Park when it was time to enter another one that promised to be just as spectacular, if not more so. I also met another cyclist called Eric. A sixty years old Canadian, he had been cycling for about a month, starting from the Mexico-Arizona border. His sunburned and blistered forearms told the story of long hot days spent crossing the desert. Our next destination was Bryce Canyon, world renowned for its crimson-coloured hoodoos, spire-shaped rock formations. The old ticker was not producing the usual goods. I felt somehow tired and weak. I realised that I was cycling above a two thousand metres plateau and would be doing so for the rest of the day. I needed time to accustom to these high altitude efforts.

After hours of peacefully riding along empty roads, I heard loud sirens behind me. Looking behind I saw a car with flashing lights and yellow flags flapping. Was it the Zion police chasing me in order to cash the entrance fee to the park? As a cyclist I had taken the liberty of letting people with engines do the paying. The noisy convoy approached and I had just moved to the side as two large villas on wheels overtook me. I looked with some astonishment as kitchen, bathroom, bedrooms, front door and windows raced past me.

Isolated farms had large signs with names of clans, such as 'Duke Hayken Clan'. Unlike their Sicilian counterparts, I hoped the meaning on this occasion would rather be religious than criminal. Up to 1890 Mormons could marry several wives.

- Bryce Canyon, Utah, USA -

One can imagine how, with such lack of entertainment, things might get out of hands. One planned having a family and before long ended up having a clan. At a good burger place in Hatch, I met Kathleen from Las Vegas and her nephew Robert. They were excited to hear about my journey and insisted I should join them at their table. We shared contacts and took pictures together with and without bike. They were heading for a day in Bryce themselves.

"Are you sure you don't want a ride in the car?" asked Kathleen.

"No thanks. That would be cheating."

"I won't tell..." she said.

I loved being out in the open, experiencing my journey to the full, one pedal stroke at a time. I would not have traded my luck for anything in this world. We parted and I had a little relief knowing that if I ever got stuck in the middle of nowhere I had a phone number to call. Having reached North camp at Bryce Canyon, a clear signpost informed all visitors that it was full. I begged the campground ranger and in the end was allowed to pitch my tent on a site usually reserved for park employees. The location couldn't have been better. A short walk brought me to the edge of a rim, staring down at a mesmerising view.

I was in a most unusual and special place and I granted myself the luxury of a couple of days in order to explore it. I cycled three thousand metres further up to Rainbow Point Loop, taking in the grand views of the canyons and hoodoos. Days living at high altitudes had turned me into a sturdy sherpa, red blood cells thick and lungs of gold. Bronte rose impervious through the barren landscape, sporting a new Utah registration plate. 'Utah, Life Elevated, X80 1BY'. My ecological twist on this trip included Solar panels sitting on top of my front bag. With constant sunshine, they worked wonders and kept my gadgets alive as well as bouncing off a healthy tan onto my face. Light continuously transformed the shapes and colours of these canyons. They were at their best when the sun was rising or diving low before sunset, casting long shadows.

After a day on my own I rejoined Eric. He let me share his huge campsite spot, and the following morning I returned the favour by treating him to a breakfast buffet at the local hotel. The man was as large as his appetite. He made the most of the 'eat as much as you like' offer. Helping upon helping fast piled up on his plate. Bacon, eggs, potatoes, sausages, bread, fruits, yoghurt. Offering buffets meals to cyclists is always a loss making enterprise. I did my best too, stuffing myself to the brim.

We stumbled out of the front door a little overwhelmed by the fast calories intake. I wondered whether I would be able to sit on my bike, let alone pedal.

- Grand Staircase, Utah, USA -

Eric's strength astounded me. In his sixties he had an imposing bear like figure. He was two metres tall with a sizeable protruding belly: hardly a cyclist's physique, one might say. Despite this he would set off in the early morning, disappearing into the far distance, never to be seen again for the rest of the day. Once more he got on his bike and sprinted ahead of me, leaving me no chance of keeping up. In the cold air of the morning I gasped for breath, overwhelmed by a cumbersome digestive struggle.

I wondered whether he was hiding an electric engine of some sort. Later that afternoon, with steep hills rising, for the first time I spotted his figure growing larger and larger in front of me and finally caught up with him. A little tired, he was still pulling his spare pounds up steep hills with brute force and shear determination. He had recently divorced and was cycling away from his ex-wife, and he told me how he had never been so happy in his life. As a prison officer he was trained not to trust and to be wary. I found out that he carried a selection of weapons such as a large hammer, a knife and assorted cans of pepper sprays.

"Mostly for bears. I keep them right by my side in the tent." he said.

"You just never know what could happen."

Living in close contact with convicts, he was ready to snap at any moment and fast. I made sure to never approach his tent without a clear call and ample warnings.

After the wonders of Zion and Bryce, cycling had become almost ordinary until, after a straight climb up the highest point of the day, I found myself in front of the vast expanse of the Escalante Staircase. Down below me as far as the eye could see, was an alien landscape of flat rocks and smoothed out large stones. I was about to dive down and cycle it to the end. I couldn't help feeling small and vulnerable. In the evening Menno finally caught up with me at the campsite. Due to his poor health, he had decided to rent a car instead and follow me for part of my journey. He had been most unlucky and wanted to at least experience some of the sights he would have loved so much to cycle.

A further climb to almost three thousand metres lead me downhill to the town of Torrey. Every now and then, in the middle of nowhere, I would spot Menno's white Ford parked by the side of the road. It was reassuring to know someone in the midst of such remote landscapes. In the boot of his car he carried an ice box where packs of chilled coke cans were neatly stowed. In a couple of days I would be starting to ride through some pretty arid land. I mused on being served gin and tonics and sodas in the middle of a dry desert. Menno was aware of my obsession with registration plates.

"You know, I really like your Nevada plate." I once remarked innocently.

"Yes it is rather nice." he replied.

"It's a rental car. Just promise me you won't pinch it."

Heading towards Hanksville was like gate crashing a John Wayne movie set on a bicycle. I waved goodbye to Menno and my mini bar fantasies. Adding to the long list of misfortunes, his rental car's dashboard had now started flashing warning lights. Being in a rather remote corner, he thought it wise to find a rental place and change the car. He had definitely learned acceptance and carried on with the patience of a saint. Outside Torrey was the entrance to Capital Reef National Park: more spectacular cycling laid ahead. The road passed by a red sandy desert, before twisting and turning at the bottom of large granite vertical rocks. I had a bit of a scare too when I suddenly heard a frantic scuffling noise in the bushes by the side of the road. Two large turkeys, who hadn't heard my quiet engine, scrambled out in front of me, terrified as if Christmas was approaching.

I also met President Carter, although I will never know for sure. In one of my frequent stops to admire the views, I chatted to this man with a southern accent and a slow paced voice. He looked remarkably like the real man but was also wearing sunglasses, and I didn't have the guts to ask for his name. Back to John Wayne. I stopped in the only café I could find along the road and discovered that he had indeed shot some of his movies not far from here. The café's walls were full of his portraits, some of them signed too. I was told he visited the place often and was friends with the owner's grandpa; the battered rocking chair, displayed in the corner, had been brought by him because he liked a comfortable chair to sit on when taking breaks.

Traffic was sparse and any signs of life rare. In these vast stretches of desert and canyons, I imagined what an easy prey I would have been for a bunch of Navajo Indians setting their chase. Not the slightest chance I thought. I would have surely fainted well before any arrows were shot.

- Escalante, Utah, USA -

I was surrounded by a desolate landscape, immersed in a silence broken only by the faint whistles of a gusty wind. I had to ration my water, taking small sips as I knew it would take hours to find some more. No wonder that, a few miles from here, a Mars Laboratory had existed for decades, simulating ways to cope with life on Mars. It was beguiling yet harsh. The reaction of those few people I met along the way spanned from admiration and encouragement to a firm conviction that on a flimsy looking bike like this, I must be completely insane. After three sweaty days managing on baby wipes, dialogues with strangers were getting shorter and shorter too. I dreamt of being able to take a good shower and wished that some enterprising person had realised the marketing opportunities of extra large, grown up wipes too.

Menno's news reported further struggles with bad customer service in remote rental car places. Armed with a tub of Nutella, two large loaves of bread, mixed nuts and berries and as much water as I could bring, I set off for the toughest few days of the journey. I had to cross two hundred kilometres of dry desert and canyons with zero facilities and lots of maybes. Before leaving Hanksville and diving into that emptiness, I stopped by the local ranger's office to seek some reassurance. Ominously, it also functioned as a medical and first aid centre.

I asked whether I would find a few drops of drinking water along the way. The welcoming ranger lady stared at a large map hanging on the wall shrugging her shoulders and with negative head shakes. All that was certain was that there was a tap of water with a little shop in Hite Marina, about a day away.

"Is the shop open?" I asked with some trepidation.

"Well...I haven't been there for a long time and that place is a little unpredictable, but ....it should be."

"I can ring up if you want?" she continued.

"Please do...!"

The phone call was promptly answered. There was water there and a little food shop too.

Chances of survival were improving.

I was clinging to Hanksville, wary of leaving civilisation behind. I stopped next at the gas station, asking if I could soak my hat under a water tap and get a fresh start to my day.

The guy behind the desk had some advice.

"You can buy a special collar that you can soak to keep cool during desert hikes. Same material as diapers. It keeps your neck and ears cool." he said.

I was getting enough attention I thought. There was hardly any need to be cycling around a desert with a soaked diaper wrapped around my head. Like an apprentice swimmer trusting the water on his first deep dive, I started pedalling along the straight road that seemed to end nowhere. After a few hours and a total of two or three cars passing by I heard some honking behind me. It was Menno. He was driving a new black rental car. With a re-supplied cooling box, he had made it his mission to rescue the half dozen crazy cyclists baking on the highway that day. It was rather lonely out there and each time a cyclist approached from the opposite side there was a definite stop and instant bonding.

- Canyonland National Park, Utah, USA -

I first crossed two remarkably fit ladies in their seventies followed by a German guy called Willie. I asked him how much water he was carrying. I felt an amateur and totally unprepared. He was carrying a staggering amount of liquids that included five litres of water and, rather oddly, zwei liters of milk too! Next was Chris who, unlike the others, was going in the same direction as me. He was a Californian in his fifties, full of life. Years of cycling all over the States meant that he knew all the shortcuts to get anywhere quicker than the rest of us cycling on regular roads.

It proved a pretty tough day and I reached Hite Marina a little late. The shop lady who had answered the phone-call in the early morning, kindly extended her opening times and welcomed me with a free mug of coffee and all the tap water I could drink. Chris, Menno and I had a good chat about our day's adventures before pitching our tents on the sand. After a spectacular sunset behind the western canyons, bright stars lit the desert sky.

The second day through the desert proved to be even tougher. Chris, knowing better, had left first, setting off at five am. I left about an hour later. We both tried to gain ground in the early morning when temperatures were cooler. After one hour of riding uphill in a fierce headwind that made progress slow and painful, I spotted Chris' bike thrown by the side of the road. He was lying next to it, black sunglasses covering his eyes, still as if he was dead.

"Chris, are you ok?" I shouted, thinking he might have collapsed and taken a fall.

He woke up from a deep sleep.

"Hey! I am fine." he said, getting up while wiping off the sand.

"I thought you might have taken a fall or something..."

"It isn't the best place to have an accident."

"Man, I tell you something." said Chris.

"If you ever catch me by the side of the road in a dire state, promise me you will twist my neck and kill me there and then."

"I have lost all private insurance and could never afford the bills."
Such is the state of American Public Health.

We were the only cyclists on the road that day. Menno stopped with the car a couple of times, offering unlimited coke cans. The lack of any water or shop to restore one's energy or even a place to briefly sit down in the shade made progress harder. At the end of a gruelling eleven hours ride, I was finally relieved to get back to civilisation in the little town of Blandings. On the last three steep climbs before reaching the town I pushed the bike, exhausted and a complete wreck. It had taken hundred and thirty kilometres of total desolation, a thousand metres climb in a blustery wind blowing right in my face. Gusts had been so strong that I had to cycle even down the steepest of hills. Chris never made it to town, but he carried a tank of water and lots of food. Surely he had wisely decided to call it a day much earlier, resting in his tent in the middle of nowhere, completely free.

That evening I met Elijah, who was cycling across America from San Francisco to Virginia. He had been granted some kind of sponsorship from the owner of a Japanese company in the energy drink business. The deal was that his expenses would be covered provided that he lugged around two large bags of white powder. What he also had to do was update the company's social media page with a blog of his travels. To ensure they would not suddenly cut all funds his entries were obviously egging the benefits of the mysterious drink. It seemed too good to be true. I wondered whether he had been set up by a drug dealer instead, unwittingly carrying illegal substances from coast to coast.

The following morning, as I was about to set off from Blanding, I heard my name shouted loudly from across the road, an unusual event in Utah. It was Chris, my newly appointed cycling guru. Unlike me the previous day, he emerged from the canyons in style, as always good humoured and full of life. He had left earlier that day to get to Blanding and was now determined to call it a day to rest his legs and do some spring cleaning.

I asked him to keep cycling and join us.

"Oh man, I can't go on like this." he said.

"It's about time I get a proper wash and do some laundry."

"If I don't, someone along the road will soon stop me, tackle me to the ground and set me on fire."

I was a little sad to leave him behind, but I had to follow my plans and keep going, crossing into Colorado. I had already recovered a State license plate by the side of the road and was ready to fit it on Bronte when the appropriate time came. Utah had left me completely in awe with all its National Parks and astounding landscapes. It was time to give Colorado a chance. The new State introduced itself with unexpected flat farmlands, but a few hours of cycling were enough to spot the first hills in the distance and, once I reached Dolores, snow capped mountains loomed ahead. I was still riding on a high plateau and, before starting the real climbs, I was already at more than two thousand meters and out of breath.

Large animal carcasses were a common sight by the side of the road. My imagination ran wild debating what kind of animal could have chewed them so neatly, down to the bones. With all the cows roaming free, there was a great choice of food around. Reassuringly lean and trimmed after all this cycling, I would surely make a rather unlikely choice. Late in the day a four wheeled preacher overtook me as

I slogged up the mountain. His diesel pickup puffed black poisonous fumes, pulling a trailer holding a large advertisement board. On it was a message in large bold fonts saying that 'Jesus Saves'. All I could think of was that 'Gasoline Kills'.

Quaint Dolores was not as painful as its Spanish name implied. It was a pleasant mountain village in between seasons; summer almost over, while the snow was yet to come. It looked really familiar to me, not unlike a typical Alpine resort. The road followed the Dolores River along a narrow valley with a gentle climb up the 2400 metres of Priest Gulch. Here the elegant campsite made for an ideal stop for the night. I was just enquiring about prices when Menno walked into the little store. I hadn't seen him the whole day. He had got involved in passionate conversations with other bike enthusiasts he had met along the way. We found an idyllic spot to share, metres away from the fast flowing river and its soothing lullaby. The following day, Menno's plans involved a long drive to Pueblo in order to meet some friends.

- Lizard Head Pass, Colorado, USA -

I hoped he would soon be able to get on his bike and do what he so much loved to do. He had been a great support along the way and his cool cans in the desert would be thoroughly missed.

In the high mountains, temperatures were now falling below zero, a far cry from the constant heat of the desert. I slept the night wearing everything I carried. In the early morning, after losing the battle with a chilly night, I rushed to the warmth of the laundry room to regain full use of my limbs. I waved Menno my last goodbye and began to climb Lizard Head pass. At over three thousand metres, this was the highest place I had visited with Bronte or any other bike.

The landscape was transformed. Dry deserts, canyons, granite peaks and scrubs had given way to a more familiar landscape. It felt as if I was back on the other side of the Atlantic, cycling over some Swiss or Italian Alps. Food portions reminded me I was still very much in America. In the mountain village of Rico I sat at a café and was served half a chocolate cake. Next was the pulled pork sandwich at the Mercantile in Sawpit. It was a giant size loaf with shredded pork dripping in a tasty sauce. It had been highly recommended as one of the best in the country.

On a bike I love the freedom of not quite knowing where I will end up sleeping at night. Having reached Placerville I was determined to test the local Fire Brigade. I had heard that in the US they are mostly welcoming to strangers and offer a bench or space for a tent on their lawn. However, the fire station that I had marked on my map was eluding me and was never found. I saw the Sheriff's car parked by the side of a road crossing and asked for some advice.

"Officer, would you know a safe place where I can pitch my tent for the night?"

"Just go straight outside the village and you will find a trail on the left," he said.

"Follow the trail about half a mile and you'll find a good place."

"Nobody will bother you there. Stay safe."

"Just watch out for bears and cats as they have been recently spotted in the area..." he continued.

I thought he wasn't talking pets. Putting on a brave face I wanted to know a little more.

"You mean mountain lions?"

"Yeah." Came the quick reply.

I steadied the jitters and dug deep for oxygen.

"That's fine I'll store my food away from the tent..."

Nothing was fine but who else could I trust if not the sheriff.

I reached the trail, found the spot he meant but on close inspection I was horrified. Littered with hundreds of spent bullets, it looked like a favourite county firing range. Hardly a sensible place to pitch my tent, never mind the cats... I decided to continue up the mountain instead. As daylight grew dimmer and dimmer I finally noticed a bonfire on a large private property lawn. A man sitting by the fire waived at me from the distance. It was a clear signal, it was just meant to be. I went through the gate, introduced myself to Tim and his wife Hazel and casually asked if they knew a place I could pitch my tent. "Right here!" they said enthusiastically. I pretended to look surprised by such generosity but must admit it was exactly the answer I had been waiting for. We had a nice conversation keeping warm by the fire and I was even offered dinner, which I refused as I was still trying to digest the pulled pork.

Cycles of frost, thaw and baking heat continued. That night in Tim's lawn it dropped below zero. The following day, only a few hours later, I crossed the mountains and under a scorching sun reached the lovely town of Ridgway. I was very much in America. In the local park a grandpa well into his seventies was teaching his niece how to skateboard and be cool. People around here were most friendly. In each little town I stopped in, strangers would start a conversation. They told me all the good places I should go and see. I regretted not having the time. Over a thousand kilometres had passed and I had only a few hundred left to go. Bronte never likes big roads and she tells me gently, usually by means of punctures. The first one of this trip happened right outside a little café and could be repaired over an ice cream.

Climbing the hills outside Montrose, I noticed a man vigorously waving at me in the distance. As I approached I was amazed to recognise the familiar figure of Chris. Our paths had crossed again. He should have been a day behind but there he was, grinning with a can of coke and crisps in his hand. He stopped for hours chatting with strangers, swam in the lakes, kneaded and baked his own sourdough bread, took generous naps along the highway, rode a heavy bike full of bags. Quite how he could still be ahead was beyond me. I was really happy to see him again.

He hated Trump and loved to have a bash at him, sharing his frustrations with foreigners he met on the road.

"Man, I just can't have this sort of conversation with Americans." he said.

"Some assholes still support him around here... you never know..."

"You know...I have a dream." he said.

"Next year I am going to take the whole year off and cycle around the world. It will be my apology tour."

"I'll go from town to town to tell the world I am sorry."

At Elk Creek campground, on a high dry Mesa by an artificial lake, we were joined by Dave. He wore an adapted cycling helmet with an edge all around to provide some shade. We named him 'the brim'. Chris was an old hippy at heart. Having crossed into Colorado, he couldn't wait to try some psychedelic cookies he had just bought from a shop the previous day. We had lots of fun chatting under a tainted sky while he waited for the biscuits to send him off to a good night's sleep. The mighty Rockies were right in front of us, and Monarch pass at 3448 metres, was by far the highest place to ascend. The road approached the pass gently in shallow grades. The town of Gunnison filled our stomachs with an edible pizza. Chris shifted his interest from biscuits and started experimenting with some spiked mints instead. Plans of a wild camp in the National Forest were called off by the dark clouds and the scents of a storm in Sargents. We opted for a safer campground instead. We had hardly pitched our tents when I heard the first few drops of rain ticking heavy on the flysheet.

The following day all that remained was the final push up to the top of the pass and the long descent down to Salida. We woke up to a blue sky restoring our energies over breakfast. We were more than ready to tackle the last miles. Legs were a little aching but there was not much left to go and I had no doubt that Bronte would have taken me all the way. I reached the top and waited for Chris. We celebrated our small achievement on top of the Continental Divide. The last image of a wonderful journey was etched in my mind like a frozen frame. Chris overtook my cautious descent singing some Italian arias out loud, his arms waving high like a Laughing Buddha dancing with the wind.

PEAKS AND LAMAS

N
W · E
S

Ladakh

Himachal Pradesh

LEH ▲
HEMIS ▲
DEBRING ▲
PANG ▲
ZING ZING BAR ▲
JISPA ▲
KEYLONG
MANALI ▲

Peaks and Lamas

After five years of adventures with Bronte one thing was certain. This little bike had unfailingly dispatched me around the world, not once leaving me stranded on unfamiliar roads. This increasing confidence on the wrong side of forty triggered a persistent thought in the deepest recesses of my brain. It involved a hippy trail on the lofty peaks of the Indian Himalayas. What better mid-life crisis destination on the planet I thought? It was not going to be a spiritual endeavour. I would not be on the search for yogis, saints or gurus; rather what I had in mind this time was a bicycle ride on the legendary Manali - Leh highway. A classic road trip and an exercise in recklessness, it climbs some of the most accident prone and highest motorable roads on earth, linking Himachal Pradesh to the remote region of Ladakh.

A decade had passed since a backpacking trip to India had taken me along this incredible road. I remember leaving Manali at an ungodly hour of the night, boarding a reinforced van that began an endless ascent of twists and turns. Our driver, his young assistant seated by his side, steered a bunch of thrill-seekers skilfully clinging to the narrow road. In the darkness of the night we were never more than inches away from cliffs, rock falls and definite gloom.

We sat scared stiff on two facing benches as the bouncing and swaying gathered momentum and our bouncy vehicle slowly ascended. After a couple of hours there was a first announcement. We had reached the top of Rohtang Pass, only the first of a series of mountain passes and high plateaus that reached above 5000 metres. At dawn, what had been only faint silhouettes of mountains, gave way to clearer views of giant peaks wrapped in snow. Most of us felt a little dizzy too, with migraines, and lungs having to work harder for oxygen.

Hemmed in and confined, I tried to snap a meagre selection of shaky pictures through fogged up windows whenever the bumpy road offered a truce.

The rollercoaster lasted eighteen hours. During the entire trip the same driver sat at the wheel, fighting fatigue by chewing unidentified leaves dispensed at regular intervals by the assistant. Sometimes we stopped and were allowed brief moments when we could step out and take in the views as well as stretch our aching limbs. I remember spotting a couple of cyclists on the road, my feelings torn between admiration and envy for the freedom they had the courage to live.

"I wish I had the guts to do that", I thought, knowing full well that I didn't.

Those memories hadn't left me and almost exactly ten years later that rhetorical statement turned into a question:

"Would I have the guts to do it now?" I asked myself.

The experience I had gained from years of cycling brought increased trust; I convinced myself that it was now or never. Going back to Manali was the only way to find the answer.

To be well prepared I decided to invest some time in a book called 'SAS Survival Skills' by aptly named author John 'Lofty' Wiseman. A former member of the British special forces, he was full of tips for those occasions when the shit hits the fan. I read a detailed description of how to kill a yak with a Swiss army knife and other gruesome survival techniques worthy of Robinson Crusoe. I discovered that I could survive on average three days without water and a staggering three weeks without food.

Some of my favourite quotes included:

'Remember you are only as sharp as your knife.'

'Animal eyes contain water which can be extracted by sucking them.'

'Do not waste blood. It is rich in vitamins and minerals, including salt. Cannibals drinking their enemies' blood found vision and general health improved, and giddy spells, induced by vitamin deficiency, cured.'

Half way through the book I gave up reading. A life brought to such extreme misery as having to rely on murder and sucking eyes for water, was not worth living. In hindsight it was all unnecessary since I managed to survive on runny lentils instead. John 'Lofty', according to best practices in the military, stressed the importance of carrying knives, thread and needles, compasses, flint rocks, fish hooks, magnifying glasses and so on. Experience taught me otherwise. Toilet rolls are what you need! Toilet paper is by far the most underrated piece of survival kit while traveling through India. Not once had it been mentioned. I would have paid to see highly trained special forces men shitting in their pants and having to wipe their arses with a thin thread.

Plans grew in pace and as it turned out an old friend showed some interest in the project. Andrea had been the person who had first opened my eyes to the exquisite joys of cycle touring. A long time had passed since our weekend rides in the British countryside and cycling holidays in France. I recalled the time when somewhere in the rolling hills of Provence I had a glimpse of what it felt like to be free. On a summer evening, as we reached a tiny village after a long day's ride, we were unable to find a bed for the night. All we could find was an upmarket restaurant that looked beyond our means and was not exactly suited to our lycra pants and cycling gear.

It was getting too dark to go any further and there was nowhere else we could have reached anyway. Trying to figure out what could be done, I was a little upset by Andrea's lack of concern.

"We'll sleep right here, under the stars." he said.

It sounded very simple but at the time I couldn't help feeling even more upset. We had no tent or sleeping bag after all. It was the last thing that I would have considered, but was there anything else left to choose?

"And by the way" he went on, "that nice restaurant down the road? We won't spend a penny for accommodation tonight, so we might as well treat ourselves to some good food."

My silent cursing continued as we entered and walked into the most elegant dining room. We were escorted to a neatly arranged candlelit table under the constant stares of a discerning clientele. We were for sure the most underdressed diners they had ever seen. After a sumptuous dinner during which I forgot all about our plight, it was back to earth, literally. We crossed the road and walked into the field, laying down on tall grasses, under a cloudless sky. In no time Andrea was snoring. I spent the night in angst, often squashing ants which had taken a liking to my face. By dawn all trace of my sour mood had vanished as we were ready to start another cycling day. In hindsight that experience opened my eyes. I learnt that accepting the limitations and the suchness of each moment was the best way to be free.

Fast forward a couple of decades and we were ready to experience "Incredible India". We landed in Delhi, a place I have visited before, but which somehow never fails to shock my soul. As usual it was an assault on the senses. Watching life go by from our taxi window, adorned by amulets and saints, was like traveling a rollercoaster of moods. Everything seemed extreme, it made me laugh one minute and brought me to the brink of tears the next. It was late at night by the time we checked in. Our hotel bore no resemblance to the attractive images that had misguided our booking. On the positive side it was a stone's throw from the bus terminal from where our bus to Manali would depart the following evening.

After a relaxing day visiting the city we headed to Kashmiri Gate station. The initial order of patient queues going through metal detectors was shattered once we passed security. On the other side was a Kumbh Mela of unruly travelers fighting for their seats. We had bought our bus tickets in advance and our only concern was making sure that Andrea's bike would come with us. Unlike Bronte, it was a regular bike with panniers and it couldn't be folded. No one could spell out any rules. As our bus approached the parking place, we fought for the best spot and managed to get to the luggage hold first. In India things start with mayhem and continue with compromise creative solutions are always found and everything miraculously works. We stuffed Andrea's bike in the cargo compartment where it quickly disappeared into a growing heap of assorted bundles. We ran to take our seats.

It was meant to be a twelve hour night journey to our destination but after sixteen we were not even near. Multiple landslides had slowed traffic to a crawl. For a few hours we hopped from tea shops to dhabas, getting nowhere. We were the only foreigners on the bus, and had to rely on our fellow passengers. They kept us abreast on the latest traffic news delivered to their mobile phones or gathered by conversations with military personnel along the road. Needless to say we heard conflicting stories. Expected arrival times ranged from eight more hours to within the next couple of days. Each time we stopped, our driver asked us to not stray too far. He never left without a hooting signal, warning of the imminent departure. After that it was the conductor's turn to walk down the aisle performing a headcount. Initially the system worked well, but after too many stops when passengers asked for their luggage back, giving up on the journey altogether, nobody knew for sure how many of us were left. The general confusion lead to the inevitable mishap. We lost Sam.

Sam, like most passengers on this bleak journey, had planned a trek in the Himalayas. He was proud to emphasise that unlike most, he was an independent mountaineer, climbing peaks without any assistance or guides. We later learnt that this was not so much the result of bravery but rather forced on him for medical reasons.

"I am seventy years old and travel agents don't let me book treks without a note from my doctor."

He had endured multiple by-pass operations and his unwavering doctor categorically refused to provide such a note.

"He keeps reminding me that mountains around here are high and that altitude kills." he sighed.

Still, to spend a weekend climbing his beloved mountains he had set off, only god knows when, from Calcutta. He communicated with his countrymen exclusively in a foreign language, English. This seemed common among well educated Indians wanting to emphasise status. The more English words they could throw into a Hindi phrase the better. He was going full blown British, risking being misunderstood in his own country. Another of Sam's peculiarities was his distaste for garlic and butter in a country indulging in spices and ghee. Each time our bus stopped he set off on a long search in order to meet his impossible dietary requirements. It was during one of these stops that he ventured a little further than he should have. The driver switched on the engine, gave a quick horn blow and off we went. The conductor, by then exhausted, had given up counting. Our stop and go continued up the mountains for twenty more minutes before grinding to a halt behind the long traffic queue. Looking outside the window I noticed a motorbike overtaking us. Seated behind was an elderly passenger frantically trying to recognise his estranged bus, white hair fluffing in the wind. He anxiously waved for the driver to stop. It was Sam. His search for garlic and butter free meals had led him astray and only sheer luck saved him. A kind Samaritan had rescued him, setting off a heroic chase. He stumbled on the bus out of breath. All gentlemanly manners gone, he had turned into a viciously angry old man.

"How can you drop an old man like that and set off with my luggage!" he screamed, emphasising the by-passes, multiple surgeries and special dietary requirements that had led him further than he should have.

Rumour spread that the road had finally reopened. It didn't feel like it. We crawled inches per hour, so slow that even a group of Tibetan monks lost their patience. They got off their bus and set off for a brisk walk, frantically shifting beads on their rosaries.

We reached Manali after a twenty hour journey with a ten hour delay. Tired, we stumbled off our bus and retrieved our bikes in a muddy parking lot under the pouring rain. Rivers of mud streamed down the steep village roads. I hadn't even started cycling but was already pondering whether I had simply been a fool. Still here I was and there was no way back.

The morning of our departure greeted us with a glorious blue sky and a break from the monsoon season with its cloudy days and pouring rain. As was always the case on these journeys, any fear of failure disappeared as soon as I sat on the saddle. A long-anticipated cycling dream was about to begin. I pushed the first few pedal strokes on the way to Rohtang Pass, our first mountain hurdle, and gruesomely translated as 'Ground of Corpses', due to the large number of casualties that occurred in the attempt to cross it. Not wanting to add to the bad statistics, we had planned to break the ascent into two more manageable days. Despite recent downpours, the road was dry. The little mud we found was of the kind that lets you float on top rather than sinking you. Cycling with Andrea I got used to being reminded of the inexorable passing of time. Each hour was marked by the single toll of a Mindfulness bell app he had installed on his mobile phone.

"It reminds me to come back to the present moment." he said.

I had my little eccentricities too. In such a remote corner, I knew it was unlikely that I would be able to cultivate my passion for car registration plates. I had decided to bring along a yellow and blue New York State registration plate, displayed at the front of my bike. Like Andrea's bell ringing regularly in his bag, my plate raised questions too. At our first village stop to get some food, the puzzled shop owner pointed to the registration plate.

"How much?" he kept saying.

I wondered whether he was asking if I would sell it. His son, with a better grasp of English, joined in and solved the impasse.

"My dad is wondering how much you are fined in your country if you cycle without a registration plate."

We were about to reach Mahri and call it a day when I heard loud explosions echoing further up the valley. All the traffic, including bicycles, shepherds and sheep, ground to a halt. More loud bangs followed. Ladakh was still far off, but I wondered if we had stumbled on an advanced Kashmiri uprising. Like on the bus, locals came to our rescue and, to our relief, told us it was road works instead.

Here a clarification is needed. Any type of construction work in India is a misnomer. Despite the country's drive to modernise, away from the big cities it was destruction that stood out. Often buildings were crumbling of their own accord due to natural causes and neglect. When these failed, an infantry of men armed with large hammers, subjected them to a constant pounding. I wondered if it was a way for

Indians to keep fit, since hammering stonewalls seemed a favourite pastime. Road works followed a similar principle. It seemed that no renewal could be effective without complete and utter destruction. Resurfacing roads was a rarity. What they did was destroy the little patches of asphalt that remained. On this occasion hammers were not up to the task and out came the mines.

This roadblock was at the mercy of a young and inexperienced mine manager. With military discipline, he wouldn't let cars, bikes, pedestrians or sheep progress an inch further. When questioned how long it would take, he invariably answered "one more explosion". After a few "one more explosions", the go ahead signal was finally given. All the traffic, that had patiently waited at both ends of the road, remembered that this was India. Long queues of cars and trucks set off from their respective sides along the single lane road. Andrea, partial to the niceties of orderly Scandinavian roads, uttered a sigh of disbelief. Inevitably they all became entangled in a mighty knot right in the middle. Progress stopped as horns and a general commotion shattered the mountain's peace. What had been a quiet Himalayan backroad, was now a traffic mess worth peak time Delhi. Mahri, halfway up the mountain, was to be our stop for the night. Despite being set in wonderful surroundings, it was not much more than a parking lot. A few tents and dhabas offered the only chance for a bed, some lentils and a cup of chai. Majestic views were hidden by dark clouds, the faint light of the approaching night adding to the dreary feel of the place. It started drizzling too, but it had been a wonderful day of cycling and we had no reason for complaint.

In the morning we woke up to another day of clear blue skies. A stray dog I had spotted during a visit to the small stupa started trotting along, following our bikes. After a couple of hours and twenty kilometres stuck to our wheels, he reached the top with us. At almost 4000 metres, tongue lolling, he called it a day and collapsed in the shadow of the pass marker, as if wanting to emphasise his feat.

If it had been food he was after he was left disappointed. All we carried were bags of nuts, sultanas and Andrea's hard, dry apricots with stones. I also had some Japanese emergency biscuits I had brought with me in case of any mishaps, but using those so early on was out of the question. I patted Mahri, a name given out of our lack of imagination, on the head a few times hoping to cheer him up a little. He was not pleased and stared at me with a sad look in his eyes. I dropped some nuts and sultanas on a stone but a quick sniff was all it took to sink his mood even further. He went back to his patch of shadow, regretting his choice to follow such ill equipped travelers.

The spectacular weather had dissipated all my worries of rolling down Rohtang Pass in a lump of mud. I had hardly finished remarking how inaccurate the reports of bad roads were when the tarmac came to an abrupt end. A state of the art German autobahn turned into a lumpy and dusty mule track.

- Sissu, Himachal Pradesh, INDIA -

It was all downhill from there but I walked and walked, taking care not to damage Bronte. Every passing car or truck brought clouds of dust that engulfed me. Had it rained instead, I would have been wading through sludge. In Sissu we made the most of the fact that it was one of the last few chances to get a proper meal. The gargantuan dinner set off an Indian initiation of stomach cramps and unidentified rumbles. At night the flood gates opened. Andrea, who had eaten exactly what I had and had drunk water from the taps and rivers, was incredibly unperturbed. Quite a stomach. We followed the Chandra river and descended the Lahaul valley, gasping at mighty mountains rising up both sides. Andrea spotted a monastery perched half way up a steep hill.

"Let's walk up there!" he suggested with the enthusiasm of a new born baby.

On these cycling trips I tend not to waste energy in extra activities that involve too much effort and I never stray too far from roads. A quick glance at the single track climb was enough to call off a detour that would have challenged an energetic donkey.

"No thanks, I'll meet you in Tandi instead. I'll be the one sipping chai by the bridge."

I could tell Andrea was a little annoyed by the absence of any spirit of adventure. He let it be known with one of his classic hints of disapproval, which often involve what to him are unethical business enterprises. This particular time he took it out on a popular fast food chain.

"Alright, I will meet you at the McDonald's in Keylong then..."

There was no McDonald's in Keylong of course. Had there been one, after the entangled stomach of the previous night, I would have happily walked in and ordered a double Mac, Coke and fries.

Having reached Keylong, 'namaste' started mingling with 'juleh', the Ladakhi greeting that brought a smile to people's faces and an enthusiastic response. To carry all his valuables, Andrea wore an ancient pouch that was slowly disintegrating around his waist. If it was not to be thrown away, the least it needed was the attention and careful needleworks of a talented tailor. We found a shop along the main road of the village. A young lady inspected its sorry state and began the rescue operation using an old sewing machine. Andrea looked rather concerned. He had forgotten to remove his cash and hoped that he wouldn't end up with a bundle of stitched rupees.

I searched and found the last wifi signal at a travel agent. Tenzin, the owner, recommended a camp for our night's stay, of course it was his own. He later welcomed us to Jispa, where we checked into one of his tents. Life is good when the simple sight of a plastic bucket filled with piping hot water excites you. It was delivered to our tent together with another with cold water. If I was to be picky, mixing the cold water with the hot one to get just the right temperature was a bit of an art. I dowsed some too hot water with too cold scoops, until three quarters down the bucket I got the gist of it. All sweat rinsed away, we moved to the restaurant tent and munched on a filling and harmless meal.

In Darcha we were stopped at the first checkpoint and our passports were checked. Inside the little booth a military officer registered our names in a logbook. He wished us good luck before ceremoniously stretching his arm out of the window to give the rope some slack and let us pass. We acquired our next pet, a puppy dog we named Darcha. He immediately showed his affection by playing with Andrea's bike and legs. Unaware of our lack of food he decided to follow us. We crossed the bridge and started the two day ascent to Baralacha-la. The endearing puppy did not lose sight of our wheels for the entire day, coming to the rescue if either of us was lagging behind. Darcha became so attached to us that each time anybody dared to come too close, he set off a passionate chase.

- Darcha, Himachal Pradesh, INDIA -

On one such occasion I decided to offer a few chocolate biscuits to a little girl we crossed on the road. The mother lowered her from her shoulder harness letting her come towards me. Darcha charged, scaring the hell out of the poor girl, but luckily didn't bite. In Patseo we set up our tents for the first time, getting used to the altitude and breaking an otherwise long climb. We had our meagre dinner by the lake and shared our precious Japanese emergency biscuits with the dog. He liked them so much that he started to chew through our tents to get some more.

If you are considering camping with a puppy, don't. It proved challenging to say the least. Darcha loved our company and at night was not happy to rest outside the flysheet of my tent. Every time he heard signs of life inside, he looked through the transparent mesh before launching an attempt to pierce through with his extended paws.

Lots of "No Darcha, no...!" pierced the silence of the night in an attempt to stop such exuberance.

My tent was put through a quality assurance test like no other. I was in awe at how such a thin material could withstand this repeated abuse unscathed. We had pitched tents metres away from an idyllic but very gushing stream. I had questioned Andrea about the possibility of a flash flood tearing through our camp during the night. His answer had been an authoritative "I thought about it too, but I don't think so." A noisy river metres away, a restless puppy and flood scenarios played havoc with my mind, making for a particularly restless night. In the morning I was happy to see that I hadn't been washed away and all seemed in order and dry.

I stumbled out of my tent feeling drowsy and tired, but this was only the beginning. Packing the tent with Darcha was pathetic. Each string in our tents, and the neatly arranged pouches holding our belongings, made for an ideal play ground. He loved it and couldn't believe his luck. He clenched them in his teeth and paraded them all over the place, while we stared on the verge of a nervous breakdown. Eventually a sensible rescue plan was put in place. We took it in turns to lure the puppy away from all the fun. The distraction of a little walk worked and we were able to pack anything that could still be found.

Two sleepy cyclists and a temperamental dog were soon approaching the 4000 metre barrier. We were rather worried about Darcha's fate, since our emergency biscuits were running out fast and there was only one final village left ahead. If he followed us much further into the mountains he would end up stranded. Given the staunch loyalty shown over the last two days, it was hard to imagine him giving up on us easily. He never stood more than a few metres from our spinning wheels and bravely defended our territory to the point of chasing large lorries. Whenever we stopped he would sit in front of our bikes, eyes and ears scanning left and right for any possible threats or danger. We also felt some inevitable attachment, but knew that the best chance of Darcha giving up a strong addiction to our biscuits, was to take a long stop at the last few yurts of Zing Zing Bar.

As soon as we reached the tents and the couple of stone houses our wish was answered. The puppy started to inspect the new turf and discovered a lot of possibilities. At last there was a kitchen there, and more food than we could ever carry, and most exciting of all, a flock of hens was roaming free in the backyard. We had our lunch in one of the rundown tents, Darcha still faithfully sitting at our feet pondering the options. We later took a short walk and upon returning realised that the puppy had taken the right decision and had disappeared. We began climbing the 4800 metres of Baralacha-la on our own, hoping Darcha would be well looked after.

Andrea, unlike me, is an inquisitive kind of guy who loves his facts and figures. During our first week he had been particularly talkative, often asking for my opinion. Topics ranged from crop rotation on the Himalayan plains, to social issues and the status of women in Ladakh and Kashmir. I didn't have a clue and acutely felt my limitations, thanking the increasing lack of oxygen for coming to my rescue. As we cycled higher Andrea became increasingly introverted, ascending the steep mountains in a religious silence worthy of a Carthusian monk.

I was happy to save my breath as my heart was thumping like a beat machine about to blow. A large truck, toppled over on its side by a sudden landslide, was a reminder of how thin a rope life can be. Nature here was untamed and rugged, we had to step through it with care and always be on our toes. We approached the first few water crossings, which I had carefully marked on my maps. Despite months spent pondering the problem, the best I was able to come up with was a plot that involved a set of plastic bags I carried to India especially for this task. I wore them over my socks, tied them with some straps and put on my sandals. I started wading into the water which started seeping through and soaking my thick socks. The plan had miserably failed to keep the water out.

- Sarchu, Ladakh, INDIA -

Even more humiliating was the fact that those same bags were now keeping the water sealed in, sloshing around long after the river had been crossed. Andrea was riding a more suitable bike with thick tyres and could cross the river with it and laugh at my plight.

A little further along, the road completely disappeared in a mess of rivulets flooding the entire valley. A few cars had been abandoned, marooned in the gushing waters, while most of the bikers were waiting for the sun to dry their feet and boots. A crowd gathered along the few resisting banks, wondering how on earth they were meant to cross such a shambles in their regular cars. Others couldn't wait to show off their prowess at the wheel of trucks and four-wheel drive vehicles. Everybody was also a spectator, watching each attempted crossing in the hope that something would go really pear-shaped and end in a good splash.

I had no choice but to push the bike, which at least made me less likely to embarrass myself in some epic tumble. I was a little annoyed at Andrea, who had ventured up a slope in search of an illusory dry path. That set off an adrenaline rush that spurred me on to brave the currents without too much fuss. Little by little I walked my way across, eventually finding a faint reappearance of the interrupted road. Andrea followed a little later admitting defeat. In the end he had also walked across that mess getting his feet wet. Dorjee's Camp at 4250 metres, was the highest place we had spent the night so far.

The following day a recently resurfaced road descended through the most amazing scenery. We followed the Tsarap river, with its unusual rock formations shaped by strong winds, before reaching Sarchu and the border between Himachal Pradesh and Ladakh. I remembered well these landscapes. Ten years before, my jeep had stopped here giving me a brief chance to snap a photo or two. Now it was so much different and intimate. I was free and unhindered under an incredible lapis lazuli sky.

We filled our stomachs as best we could with yet another meal of lentils and rice, before spending the early afternoon riding down a valley through red mountains of sand. We were at the foot of the renowned twenty one switchbacks of the Gata Loops, heading towards Nakee-la. By loop number two my stomach was once more in tatters. I left the road, holding in one hand my precious paper roll, and searched for a sizeable rock to hide behind. Andrea overtook my parked bike at the side of the road.

"Is everything alright?" he shouted.

"Just great" I answered, in the midst of a revolution in my bowels.

Later, I was back on my bike and could see Andrea sprinting far ahead, climbing the steep road as if his lentils had been of a different kind. Now well above 4500 metres, I stopped frequently to drink and snack while he soldiered on in the far distance. I caught up with him about half way up, where he was crawling along at walking speed and looking poorly. He told me he hadn't felt too well since the previous night, when he had woken up out of breath, feeling his heart pumping hard, and a little achy.

We were almost at the top of the pass and dusk was fast approaching; hardly a good time or place to feel unwell. We slowed down and often walked, hoping a car would pass by, but for a good half hour there were none. Eventually we decided it was best to turn around and go back downhill to a lower altitude. As Andrea gradually felt better we kept going down a little further. There was nowhere near to get to, but finally a few cars were spotted climbing up from the valley. We stopped each one of them until a spare seat was found. Another car offered its roof to take Andrea's bike. I asked for some spare water before the cars left for Pang, where an army medical centre would offer him some help and advice. I pitched my tent alone, feeling rather sad about what had happened and hoping that in the following days he would be able to continue his journey.

Early the next morning I was cycling back up along the same road, on my own for the first time. I reached the top of Nakee-la and was mobbed by a group of Singaporeans keen on selfies. They lined up one at a time for the privilege of a picture with me. I dived down to the tents of Whisky Nullah, under a sky that for the first time on this trip had turned the colour of lead. Just before reaching the camp it started to drizzle. I stood still in the middle of the road, three tents to my right and three tents to my left. They functioned as makeshift restaurants and their respective owners were keen to compete for the only customer around. They all stared at me from their respective entrances awaiting a final decision. To make matters more complicated they had identical menus mostly comprising variations of lentils and rice or instant noodles.

For the first time ever on a bicycle I was above 5000 metres at the top of Lachung-la. Expectations of an enjoyable descent were frustrated by a terrible road that had me walking for twenty kilometres instead. A few kilometres before Pang I spotted a lonely figure seated by the river bank. Given the perfect location I had no doubt it was Andrea waiting for my arrival. Later I was pleased to hear that the doctor had given him the all clear. He was feeling much better and was keen to get back on his bike and start riding again. As for Bronte, it had somehow coped with rough river crossings and miserable roads for days on end, yet still looked totally unscathed.

Only one more major mountain stood between us and Leh. A couple of days ahead, Tanglang-la was the highest pass of them all. After a week of riding high mountains, by now I knew that I was well adapted to the altitude and sufficiently fit. All those worries I had carried with me since the start in Manali had one by one vanished, dropped off along the road, considerably lightening my load. I felt completely at peace with the raw nature of these remote mountains. For a few fleeting days I was invited to be part of it all, immersed and at one with such beauty.

A steep climb out of Pang brought us to the arid stretch of the Morey Planes. A narrow, black strip of tarmac, empty of any traffic, cut through the middle of a barren landscape. Only the strongest gusts of wind interrupted the complete silence. A few shepherds tending their herds could be seen in the distance, while the occasional group of motorbikers sped through. Our last host in Pang had recommended we stop in Debring, a little cluster of half a dozen nomad yurts where her granny lived. She wrote the name 'Jigme Dorjee' on a piece of paper and assured us that we would be welcomed like family and have a comfortable stay. We arrived at the tents in the early hours of the afternoon, for once happy to settle down early after an easy day's ride. We showed our invitation card in one of the yurts and were directed towards tent number three.

Expecting a good natured elderly grannie to welcome us we found a young chap instead. His name was Dikshit, but in his mumbling pronunciation it sounded much more like Biscuit. This was easier to remember too and reflected the jolly nature of his character. It was hardly two in the afternoon, but Biscuit already showed some signs of being tipsy.

"That's my mom!" he said reading our piece of paper.

"She is not here these days but I am, my friends! You are welcome to stay."

We had our doubts but Biscuit was extremely endearing and friendly. He showed us to a cosy extension at the back of his Yurt where thin mattresses had been laid on the floor covered by a thick layer of carpets. Andrea was keen to have a nap and, having cycled for many days without interruption, I was happy to lie down too. Later I wandered around the tents basking in a warm afternoon sun, while Andrea set off a little further on one of his adventurous walks. Biscuit, despite being by now completely stoned, managed to cook us some dinner with a constant grin painted on his face. While we were still eating he announced he had some errands to do and left for about thirty minutes. He returned with a broad smile and a full bottle of whisky under his arm, telling us that life was so good. He offered us some, but the lack of oxygen was enough to make us dizzy. After sunset we hid in our little tarpaulin alcove and called it a day. It was going to be an interesting night. Around two am we were woken up by people talking loudly and by some repetitive noise of metal banging. A little later a diesel car engine was started and left running with the exhaust pointing right into our tent. I thought I was either having a bad dream or someone was trying to kill us. Whatever it was, Andrea and I agreed that it was definitely not doing our lungs any good.

"Biscuit!" I shouted "What the hell is going on?"

More wasted than ever, he could only reply with mumbles and short syllables and sounded confused.

"Let me...find out...Sorry...Sorry..."

All he had to do was look behind the tent and see whose brilliant idea it was to have a running engine spewing poisons in our tent in the middle of the night.

Andrea started dwelling on conspiracy theories that covered all the worse case scenarios. Was it manslaughter or robbery? We were the only two foreigners in a remote corner of Ladakh after all. What were we supposed to do? As for myself, I couldn't breathe in any more fumes and knew exactly what I had to do. I went outside, dragging a heap of blankets and carpets, and laid down on a couple of plastic tables. I hid in my sleeping bag, trusting in the good nature of Buddhists and their belief in Karma. It was my turn to accept all limitations and peacefully rest under the brightly lit stars. Andrea was having none of this. After many trips in and out of the yurt assembling his gear, he wanted to take off fast on his bike, cycling up a mountain in complete darkness.

"We must leave!"

"You just go if it makes you feel better. I'll start cycling once I can see where I am going and catch up with you later." I said.

"How can I leave you alone like this..." he continued.

Biscuit was now also frantically toing and froing. Incredibly he hadn't yet figured out what was going on.

"Sir...you sleep outside???" he wobbled, concerned.

"You bloody bet I am. Do you want me to die? I can't breathe in there!"

It was still the middle of the night but Debring camp was now wide awake. Generators were started and lights were turned on. Sleepy faces peered through yurt doors, intrigued by the idiosyncrasies of two foreigners. One lying on their plastic tables in the courtyard while the other one was pacing up and down the main road like a Royal guard on night patrol.

At dawn we tried to wake up Biscuit in order to pay him for the terrible night. Our efforts failed, despite our shouting and shaking he lay seemingly dead on a sofa. We left what was due minus twenty percent for the attempted murder and inconvenience and started to climb the 5300 metres of Tanglang La . Andrea was a little concerned after his previous experience with altitude, but taking his time he managed to cycle all the way up. Celebrations of our achievement were brief, cut short by the chilly winds.

- Hemis, Ladakh, INDIA -

We could have reached Leh in a couple of days had we wanted to, but as a way to end this trip we decided to spend a couple of days in Hemis monastery instead. One of the main Tibetan Buddhist complexes in Ladakh, I had fond memories of its secluded location, perched on a rocky hilltop with grand views of the Indus Valley. At that time I had been travelling on a motorbike and had forgotten how steep the access road was. It was quite a ramp that would have made for a perfect skiing slope. We pushed our bikes and bags, huffing and puffing for most of the way, a true test for the faithful.

The monastery's guest house was full so we opted to spend two nights at Chunpa, a home stay managed by a Ladakhi family, just below the entrance gate. We were welcomed into their kitchen, where they offered us mint tea and some freshly cooked bread. The owner's daughter, on a summer break from her Delhi university studies, was busy cooking dinner. Her aunt sat in the far corner whispering Buddhist prayers while running beads through her hand. We put an end to our diet of lentils with a delicious meal of vegetables freshly picked from the garden and spent a joyful few hours chatting with the assembled family.

After dinner we moved upstairs ready to get some sleep when I spotted the largest spider I had seen since my last visit to the London Natural History museum. Unlike the museum specimen, this fellow was happily moving about. He was dangling from the wooden beams one minute while crawling along the thick curtains above my bed the next. We were in a Buddhist Ladakhi house and a good flattening bang seemed out of the question. I ran downstairs instead to ask for some help. Half the family got involved in the delicate effort to shift the monster out of the window without any harm. It was hopeless; teased with a broomstick and dustpan the spider skilfully sprinted all over the ceiling, finding perfect cover in all the nooks and crannies. They didn't seem much worried. Whether this was because they were familiar with spiders or because after all it was my room, I couldn't quite tell.

I asked some questions.

"Is it dangerous? Does it bite or chew?"

They did their best to reassure me, promising that despite the mean look, it was harmless. I zipped up my sleeping bag extra tight, baptised the creepy-crawly by naming him Arthur and resigned to share my room with another pet. We had a couple of relaxing days roaming around the Gonpas of Hemis and joining the monks for their early morning chanting. On our last night our Ladakhi hosts produced their best meal so far, treating us to a heap of homemade momos and pancakes.

- Leh, Ladakh, INDIA -

Leh was only a couple of hours ride away. I recognised Thiksey and Shey palace as I passed by them along the way but once we reached the outskirts of Leh, it was clear that it had been transformed. Gone was the small town I remembered. I struggled to find something familiar, in what was now a larger city, with modern buildings and hotels sprouting from every corner. The hotel I had booked months in advance was literally still sprouting. Walking through the entrance gate we realised that the first floor and a proper roof were still missing. We pushed our bikes through a tended garden with a green lawn and beds of colourful flowers before entering the lobby, and asked if we were a little early. Next to the reception desk a flight of stairs led to a wonderful blue sky. We hadn't paid much for the room, but nevertheless hoped that it would be on the ground floor. The polite owner was full of care and reassured us that the building site had been put on halt for the time being until the tourist season was over. Our room had been finished and hopefully there would be some dry weather in the lobby. Should it rain, we could be in for a treat, admiring a remarkable waterfall flowing down the spiral flight of stairs.

For a few weeks I had been living what for many years had been just a dream. Only a reckless thought of cycling these roads, let me discover Ladakh like I had always wanted to. Cycling slowly along those valleys and dramatic landscapes, I had listened to the sound of silence, experienced the kindness of its people and forgotten any taste of fear. Back in the noise and traffic of Leh, I was half a step nearer to home already, missing the wholehearted smiles of the Ladakhi and all those 'juleh'.

CHASING COLOURS

Chasing Colours

I have always loved the colours of autumn when leaves paint mountains with variegated hues of red, yellow and green. I decided to head to New England, a world renowned leaf-spotting paradise. I had seen plenty of inspiring pictures but I was also well aware that autumn weather can be moody, comes with a temper and is not always benevolent to cyclists. It was still worth the gamble. I appointed myself inspector of a forthcoming Michelin Good Foliage Guide and set off on a mission to award golden leaves to the most deserving villages and trees.

A new journey began with an adventurous night at a Boston hostel. I checked into a small dorm shared with five persons. This time I was also better prepared than I had been in the past, bringing earplugs and eye mask, in the hope of getting a little rest. The following morning around five am, a mobile phone chime went off rather loudly. Not too annoying at first, the digital melody persevered a good ten minutes, wearing everybody's patience thin. A search began as my room mates started scanning the room to find out the culprit. From my strategic top bunk position I could see lots of crawling on all fours, as the room was inspected inch by inch. They were all trying to figure out the location, the nature but crucially, the off-switch button of the blighted instrument. It was all in vain, the carillon went on unperturbed, with punctual, five minute reminders. It was soon clear it belonged to the only person still snoring loudly in the room. Brad, from Austin Texas, was the sole intended target yet after a late night out all attempts to wake him up were failing. The general unrest ended when half asleep he somehow managed to stretch out an arm and silence it. There was a premature sigh of relief but ten minutes had hardly passed when another round of reminders began. Brad was again unaware and fast sleep. A Chinese guy on the nearby bed, patient until now, started what I assumed to be a stream of Mandarin cursing. A sense of doom and despair pervaded the room. Youth hostels consistently deliver good stories that compensate for the lack of sleep! Boston was bright and sunny and cycling around the city for most of the morning I was able to catch a few glimpses of its charm. The inspector officially set off. After the ramble around Boston, Harvard University and MIT happened to be along the way. I thought it would be interesting to stop by and be able to say that I went to Harvard without paying the extortionate fees. The leafy college yard, in a borough confusingly called Cambridge, was bustling with tourists. Proud looking students moved to and from elegant buildings carrying heavy loads of piled up books. Not all was well in the Ivy League. A noisy rattle could be heard growing louder and louder until a large protest march paraded through the gates. The main slogan, repeated over and over again, went along the lines that whatever they wanted they wanted it now... no patience whatsoever.

- Boston, Massachusetts, USA -

The continuous sprawl from Boston to Cambridge slowly gave way to the countryside, a string of quaint villages and Walden pond. Here, Thoreau wrote his most famous work and lived for two years testing self sufficiency and an idealist return to nature. Nearby was Concord, the main town in the area, its hills scattered with memorials of historic battles for independence. It also boasted an impressive literary heritage; but as far as foliage went, the town was having a bad day. The inspector, harsh as it seemed, cycled past most places rather unperturbed. As for Golden Leaves, he awarded none.

Heading north past Ayer, I took the Nashua River Rail Trail. Quite a tongue twister, but a peaceful bike path that had been suggested the previous night by my host David. It took me across an invisible border into New Hampshire. I left Massachusetts behind with a sense of relief that at least I wouldn't have to try spelling it anymore. As I entered the new State I discovered that its motto, displayed as usual on cars' registration plates, was an uncompromising 'Live free or die'. Having reached Nashua I soon wondered whether all this freedom had backfired. A large percentage of the population seemed to have twisted the slogan into a 'Live free AND die'. A lunch stop in a local mall made me realise how they munched incredible amounts of junk food and pies, washed down with complimentary buckets of soda. The result was obvious and far too many people were seriously obese. At a traffic light on Nashua's Main Street I saw the largest human being I have ever seen. A middle-aged woman crossed the street right in front of me, slouched on an electric wheelchair that seemed like rather a large sofa on wheels. She filled it with her flesh to the brim, sadly unable to carry all that freedom on her own legs. As I whisked by the State capital Concord I realised what the other big culprit was. The great invention of 'Drive-ins'. You could drive-in to eat, go to a drive-in bank, a drive-in cinema and I even noticed a sign advertising a drive-in theatre. The convenience of managing life from a comfortable chair had replaced the need to use one's legs. Like everything there was also a positive side to things. At lunch time grocery stores were dishing out free pizza samples that looked more like reasonable restaurant portions to me.

Left wanting in health, New Hampshire put a lot more passion and effort into its leaves. The judge was treated to the first hints of autumn and awarded his first Michelin leaves to the villages of New Boston and Goffstown. A little stingy, but the trip had only started and if he was to be more generous, he would soon run out of leaves. Central heating, and all the comforts one takes for granted at home, are best appreciated when lacking. The night camping in the open fields could not have been a starker reminder. It was bitterly cold, but the colours I cycled through for hours each day made any discomfort worth it. Trees were on fire, painted in all kinds of shades.

It was a Presidential election year in the country. Posters of candidates running for the presidency, senate and county were splattered all over. Displayed by supporters, their names littered houses' walls and front yards. Where there were no leaves I switched my attention to signs instead. I began running my own unofficial cycling poll. If Massachusetts seemed to favour Clinton, New Hampshire was too close to call.

After a lot of trial and error I discovered a formula that helped in finding out how long it takes to cycle anywhere. Asking how long it takes to cycle from A to B in a car-biased country like the States always ends up in complete failure. Asking how long it takes to drive from A to B instead, gets you an answer that is accurate to the minute. All that one needs to do then is to multiply the answer by 3.14159.

I paid an uplifting visit to Canterbury Shaker village. Shakers seemed a very decent lot but their numbers were waning. What remained of these inspired and hard working men and women, were the polished woodcraft works and their bare but elegant wooden houses. As far as keeping the tradition alive it was now left to three sisters in the only surviving community in Maine. In Canterbury the judge was justly excited. There was an amazing display of foliage pretty much everywhere. Definitely the best seen so far, it was granted two well deserved Michelin leaves.

- Canterbury, New Hampshire, USA -

The tail end of hurricane Matthews made it into New Hampshire, messing up my day. Nothing too dramatic unless you were cycling. The sunny streak I had enjoyed so far came to an abrupt end and I was drenched. The day had to be cut short as I sought cover in a luxurious hotel in Wolfeboro. Were it not for this dreary rainfall it would have seemed an attractive little lake town, keen to advertise that it was the first summer resort town in US history. By evening, the weatherman on TV was hopeful for the next day. I would be busking in the sun at noon, chilled at night and defrosted by the late hours of the following morning. I was approaching White Mountains National Park. Rumours overheard while enjoying hot brews at a local café claimed it was looking gorgeous this year, with colours at their peak. By dusk the storm ended as planned. Clouds parted, uncovering my expensive room view overlooking a small lake. Eager to make my premium choice worth it, I could even indulge in a breathtaking sunset while lying on my bed.

Winepessaukee lake reappeared in the early hours of the morning under a clear blue sky. Temperatures after the storm felt uncomfortably fresher too. After yesterday's washout there was a definite change of mood. Wolfeboro was eager and chirpy, with plenty of smiles to be seen and 'good mornings' to be heard. It was Columbus Day and a national holiday too when I reached Sandwich, one of the nicest villages so far. The annual Autumn Fair was on. Large crowds converged in long queues to enter the lawns with merry-go-rounds, ferris wheels, haunted castles, fried sweets and pies. I left everybody to their rides, blessed by quiet country roads. Outside Tamworth library I met John, in all likelihood sent by providence. About to reach White Mountains National Park, I had planned to take the Kancagamus Highway. John was a keen cyclist himself and wouldn't let me. He began a thirty minutes thesis on why I should take the smaller Passaconaway Road instead. These were his roads, I followed the good advice, slowly approaching the rising mountains.

Common sense disappeared in Conway. The map showed a sizeable town where I had hoped to be able to restore my energy and replenish supplies before entering the National Park. I was about to be disappointed. It turned out to be a residential area with an extreme aversion to shops and any kind of useful facilities. These were all in Conway North instead, eight kilometres further on and off my route. I felt deceived. North Conway should have been Conway while the real Conway should have been South Conway at most. After a long search I did find a little store with a limited food offering. Walking beside the short shelf I noticed a mysterious drink called Pumpkin Eggnog. I was all for pumpkins and liked the odd egg too but what was intriguing was the nog. Asking the store owner, a lovely lady of Indian origin, it was clear that despite selling it, she didn't seem to have the slightest clue. This mystery was too tempting to resist; I bought it and set off for the forest where I pitched my tent and restored my energy, preparing for the mountain climbs ahead. The concoction was thick and sweet, probably never meant to be drunk neat but unlike the New Hampshire lot, I deserved all the calories I could get. At night my stomach rumbled, probably wondering what on earth had been ingested. I woke up too, feeling a burning in my stomach that I blamed on the nog.

Whatever it was it worked like a charm. The morning climb up to the top of White Mountains went swiftly. Legs were spinning, the old lungs had enough to spare for a whistle too and there was definitely some extra umphhh. The only thing slowing me down were the many scenic points that demanded I should stop. On top of Kancagamus Pass, a crew with large cameras was shooting a television commercial. I lent them my camera and asked for their expertise in shooting a video of Bronte and me proudly reaching the top of the climb. Countless stops chatting to people and taking in the views, meant that I was far behind schedule and it was getting rather late too. I had to catch up with timetables on my tight schedule as the light got dimmer with shorter and shorter days. The rebel in me took over. I pretended to lose track of the tortuous bike route and traded it for the long and fast straights of Freeway 93, ignoring all warning signs forbidding bicycles to enter. It was getting too dark and, unable to find a decent spot, I admitted defeat and set up my tent on a grassy patch by the side of the highway. Hardly an idyllic spot, it was a complete camping failure. Earplugs couldn't cope with large trucks revving their engines up the hill in front of me. At dawn I packed my tent and sorrows and decided to find my way back to a campsite I had passed by the day before and had decided to ignore. I needed some cheering up and the warmth of a coin operated hot shower.

In the morning as the sun rose above Franconia Notch State Park I could see what had only been vague glimpses the previous day. The whole mountain was coated in bright colours. The inspector dropped to his knees, sang an hallelujah and awarded three well deserved Michelin leaves to Franconia. It would be a hard act to follow. I was running out of Egg Nog. Following a recommendation I headed to the local Mexican restaurant, where a tasty burrito was served. Littleton's laundromat returned a presentable cyclist to the roads of New England. Past More dam there was the excitement of yet another border crossing. Vermont, my third State so far loomed ahead. New Hampshire had treated us well, we had lived free and hadn't died or gained too much weight in the process. Unofficial cycling presidential polls reluctantly awarded the State to Trump.

It was a sunny afternoon when I crossed into Vermont and was welcomed by the much gentler motto of 'Green Mountains State'. All political interest had withered, since the local hero under the name of senator Bernie Sanders had decided to withdraw his candidacy. Going by all the posters on display, one would have thought he had already won the Presidency. I reached Saint Johnsbury 'Where rivers and people come together'. After last night's camping fiasco I had to change my tactics. Having found an ideal spot on the premises of an attractive farm, I patiently waited for the farmer. Anne eventually appeared. I asked if she would mind me putting my tent on her land. She kindly allowed me to, with a disclaimer:

"Just bear in mind that our large dog might spot you and want to play with you."

"Is the large dog friendly and well meaning?" I asked.

"Yes. He'll jump on you," she said "but he is very kind and affectionate..."

I quietly set up camp, ducking behind all the bushes I could find before silently zipping myself in the tent. In the morning, still mindful of the animal presence, I quietly packed up and flew down Olde Farm Road at full speed. The dog had missed his chance. New England countryside roads are quite bare. One spends entire mornings searching for a shop selling some water, a sweet pastry or any other simple food. On the other hand there is a great abundance of places selling maple syrup. By the gallon. They were all full of praise for the sticky stuff, a local pride here.

- Stowe, Vermont, USA -

It tasted nice on a few breakfast pancakes too, but it was hardly the kind of staple food I could survive on. A dignified existence demands much more than maple syrup. I needed at least a few more bakeries and cafés. Six hundred kilometres into this leafy pilgrimage, I had also been searching in vain for a registration plate. I had the bright idea of walking into a car scrapyard and asking for one.

"What do you want? Vermont?" asked the greasy boss with a goaty beard.

"That would do me fine!" I replied excited.

I had just crossed into the state and nothing else could have been more appropriate.

My man emerged from the dark recesses of his garage and produced the goods; a Green Mountain State plate, registration FRM 274. I headed south in search of yet more leaves.

In Waterbury I visited the original Ben & Jerry ice cream factory. I joined about twenty people for the half hour guided tour. We heard how Ben and Jerry had started it all. The beginnings had been humble (they are always humble aren't they?) and full of strife and, talking of clichés, involved a run-down Volkswagen van too. All very informative but rather like the protesters at Harvard, we wanted ice cream and we wanted it now. The Vermont registration plate was installed and a few drops of oil later Bronte was speeding down scenic route 100.

Green Mountain National Park was yet another spectacle of nature. According to local gossip, peak time had passed a week before but the mountain colours were still vivid and I wouldn't have known it if I hadn't been told. The inspector, after presenting Stowe and Warren with leafy awards, had to shed more for the National Park and was by now running low. I cycled down Mad River Valley. The river seemed to have overcome its quirky side and made a lot of sense instead. Near Stockbridge I met Heather, a musician who run an interesting café I spotted along the road. That night they had a live folk band from Colorado playing on the little stage in the corner. Upon asking, she allowed me to put up my tent on her ground too. I had dinner listening to some good folk music, before crossing the road into the fields and diving into my tent. A cold weather front was on the way, threatening below zero degrees temperatures. Travelling light I had to wear my entire wardrobe turning into a Michelin tyre man instead. At night, temperatures dropped and I had to resort to wearing earplugs, for the first time not to block out noise but rather to stop the cold draft from drifting through my head.

In the morning, it wasn't a pretty sight. The frozen canvas had turned what used to be my tent into a free-standing igloo. Packing in the blustery wind didn't help. The thin gloves were not enough to keep me warm. I felt prickly chills spreading through my hands, I was on the verge of frostbite. Bronte painfully unfolded with a screeching noise. To warm up I started pedalling as fast as I could. I pushed away all memories of Ben and Jerry raspberry and cheesecake ice cream, dreaming about a hot soup instead. I was put out of this misery when at last I reached my only hope of survival, a hotel called Swiss Farm Inn. I defrosted over a hearty breakfast, for once appreciating a cup of coffee more for its hand-warming qualities than its flavour. Thawed, it was time to face the outdoors again under a timid sun in a winter wonderland. The inspector declared a tie between the Green Mountains and Franconia Notch. The following night, unfazed by past traumas, in semi-darkness I descended a sloping bank and pitched my tent on what seemed a rather well trimmed lawn. By dawn it was clear that I had trespassed, sleeping on the edges of Londonderry's golf club. Not far from the fairway, I was one shot away from a third hole par. It was Sunday early morning too, so I had no time to linger and thought it best to evacuate fast.

It still felt frosty and cold. I pondered a quick conversion to the evangelicals so I could join their Sunday prayers at Our Lady of Ephesus. All the singing and central heating would have gone a long way but, clad in a fluorescent green jacket and lycra, I would have stood out like a sore thumb. The Londonderry Inn, a few miles down the road, seemed a better option. I opened their entrance door, once more stiff and on the verge of hypothermia. Brian, the owner, was not as welcoming and informed me that breakfast was only for overnight guests. I was about to reconsider Sunday mass when his lovely wife Maya walked past reception. Maybe reading hints of misery on my face, she showed who was really wearing the trousers and announced that I would be made an exception. Brian sighed and sulked.

I sat dangerously close to the most wonderful fireplace, regaining full use of my limbs. I wolfed a hearty breakfast as guests slowly trickled into the dining room, ready to start their day. Three bagels, a couple of slices of cake, fried eggs and several coffees later, I was best friends with them all. They were one by one introduced to me by the owner as they entered the room. An 87 years old man, born in the local village of Weston Vermont but resident in Colorado, was first. Every elderly person's favourite topic is to nostalgically recount the old days and convince his victim that the world is not what it used to be anymore. My man was no exception and immediately started a symposium on why standards had slipped so low.

"Look. It's so crowded around here." he complained.

"When I was a boy, there were more cows than people."

His life as a child had been hard. He described his daily activities involving gruesome tasks like castrating bulls, and that was before going to school. Going to school wasn't much fun either as he had to face a long walk daily - barefoot, even in winter.

I was spoilt in my comfort but for a few frosty days, it was all incomprehensible to me. I could only ask the wrong questions.

"Why barefoot?" I asked, as if it might have been some sort of character building exercise.

"There was nothing around here." he said.
"We had no money left for shoes." his tone rising, probably surprised by my stupidity.

How could I imagine a life I wouldn't have been able to endure for a single morning?

Next to show up was Andrew from New York City. He walked fast into the room, eager to chat as if he hadn't met a human being for weeks. He was a former New York Times foreign correspondent, now retired. Despite no more deadlines or breaking news to cover, he maintained the same restlessness nevertheless.

- Pittsfield, Massachusetts, USA -

I wondered if this was an occupational hazard or whether it was the inevitable consequence of being born in a city that never sleeps. Probably a mix of both. He had lived in London, Brazil and France, and had sailed all over the Mediterranean. I found out that he was part of a group of ex Yale graduates who used to be members of the University choir. Decades had passed, but once a year they still met up for rehearsals, performing a concert somewhere. Andrew was still thrilled by politics and excited by the Presidential election. I was rather pleased when he confirmed the accuracy of my cycling polls. Massachusetts to Clinton, New Hampshire to Trump sounded about right to him too.

"Vermont?" I asked.

"Nobody can tell. After Bernie Sanders, life ended and they just don't care anymore..." he replied.

All that chatting meant a late arrival at Woodford State Park campground. A large wooden board and a lowered metal bar left me in no doubt that the place was off season and closed. I walked past the barrier and knocked on the ranger's house playing the 'tired cyclist' card. It worked again like a charm after being reminded that the camping season was over.

"Anyway..." whispered the ranger, "just go ahead straight up that road, you'll pass a forest then turn left. You can pitch your tent there."

"Just promise me you'll leave early morning." he warned.

"My boss starts his shift at seven".

"By the way, I have never seen you or said this to you. Good night."

I pitched my tent in complete darkness, Woodford State Park all to myself. It rained most of the night, but when a tent holds it is a peaceful sound to hear. By six o'clock I was up and determined to keep my promise, leaving before the early shift patrol. I opened my tent onto a blur of thick fog. As soon as I had descended the mountain road and reached Bennington, I was happily dropping quarters in yet another tumble dry paradise. The Berkshires, where rich New Yorkers and Bostonians buy their third or fourth country pads, put up quite a show. I was not too far from the Big Apple, and it showed in the increasing numbers of New York licence plates. From what I had seen so far, they didn't make for fine mountain drivers. Used to navigating right angled blocks, they were out of their comfort zones going around mountain bends. Each time I spotted a yellow and black 'Empire State' plate, I stayed well clear. It was late for the best of the colours but a mild climate and little rain meant that the mountains were still spectacular.

I crossed back into Massachusetts and the hunt for a new licence plate was back on. In Stockbridge, while taking a rest and checking maps, I was approached by Alan, a cyclist who had toured several countries around the world. After a short conversation he offered me a stay at his place for the night, but it was not meant to be. I had been so desperate for a shower and fed up with baby wipes that the previous day I had booked a hotel room in advance.

"Do you know where I could get a Massachusetts licence plate?" I asked.

"I am not sure but I happen to have an old one in my garage if you want..."

Too tempting to refuse the kind offer, I was soon cycling up a rather steep hill to reach Alan's house, where the tin award was waiting.

- Manhattan, New York, USA -

Alan shared his suggestions on the best roads to ride into New York State, where I would catch a train for a two hours journey into the Big Apple. I crossed an unprecedented, record breaking, three State borders in a single day, and all that on a bicycle. Starting in Great Barrington Massachusetts, I cut through a corner of Connecticut, before crossing into New York and reaching the village of Wassaic. The early morning fog, pierced by rays of sunshine, was framed in some of the best pictures I had taken so far. Connecticut was an unexpected surprise too. Beautiful countryside scattered with tidy little villages and friendly folks. It was only a quick dash through the peaceful Constitution State, but two hours were long enough for the polling cyclist to confidently assign the State to Hillary. She was plastered all over the place. Ronald McDonald was nowhere to be seen.

A thousand kilometres later, a quick train transfer brought me all the way to the confusion of Harlem; I was shocked to be back in a crowd. Bronte was once more unfolded and started the long parade through Central Park.

* * *

ON THE SILK ROUTE

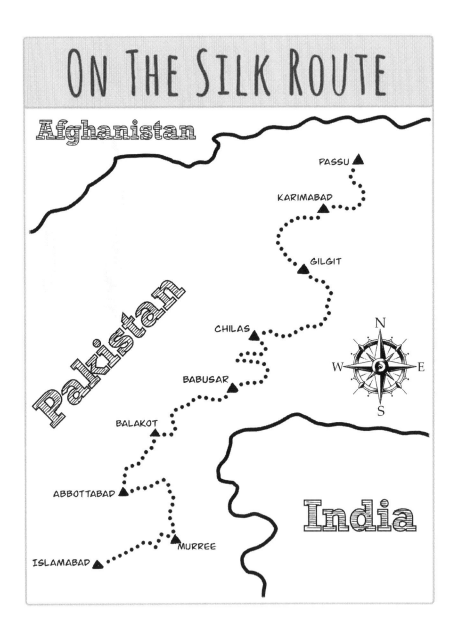

On The Silk Route

A picture on social media did it. I saw an image of a straight road and, rising vertically on the horizon, the peculiar shapes of the Passu Cones also known as the Cathedral. The road was the Karakoram Highway and the country Pakistan. I was inspired, it looked stunning but I felt uneasy. Western media has never been particularly kind to this country. Everything I had heard or read about Pakistan bar the cricket, spoke of terror attacks and looming danger. Almost a decade had passed since 9/11, yet the country was still reeling from its consequences. The thriving tourism of the eighties had come to an abrupt halt and had never recovered. Governments' advice and warnings continued; one thing they agreed on was that it was not a place for the independent traveler. Not wanting to be foolhardy, I decided to find out for myself whether there was another side to Pakistan, away from the shocking headlines and bad news. Indeed, accounts by cyclists who had recently visited told a different story. They spoke of very generous and welcoming people, and of a mostly safe country. More often than not, they expressed the wish to return.

Imran Khan, captain of the 1992 World Cup winning cricket team, was now not only a sports hero but the country's Prime Minister. Besides engaging in the endless fight against corruption and abuse of power revolving around a handful of families, he wished to open the country to international tourism once again. I made up my mind. That was where I should go next. A brand new online system promised to make the process of getting a Visa much easier. I wonder how cumbersome it must have been before!

I was requested to submit bank account statements, a letter from my employer, a detailed and fake itinerary, copies of utility bills as proof of address and hotel bookings that I would later cancel. It was not enough. A LOI or 'Letter Of Invitation' from Pakistan was also requested. This had to be issued by a Pakistani national or a recognized organisation. To limit access to those who had a kind Pakistani aunt willing to host them, seemed to go against the desire to promote tourism. Luckily, an industry of fake LOI providers was thriving. These were mostly travel agents that charged extortionate fees to write a few paragraphs of lies to allow tourists in.

I contacted Wide Horizons Treks and Tours and, upon payment, promptly received an invitation to Pakistan. It sounded too good to be true:

'To whomever it may concern, Government of Pakistan. We at Wide Horizons Treks and Tours have organised a tour of Pakistan to take place in September 2019. Wide Horizons Treks and Tours will be responsible for all of the accommodation, travel arrangements and services during the tour. We would especially like to invite Mr Gianni Filippini to join us on this trip....'

I thought I had overpaid for a fake letter but had now received an invitation to an all inclusive package tour.

I added this to my application bundle. It was not enough. I was next asked to attend an interview at the Pakistan High Commission in London. On a Monday morning I walked through the entrance and left orderly Knightsbridge behind me. I joined a half-hearted queue in front of a metal detector. It all seemed a bit pointless. Each person walking through it set off bells and red lights that didn't seem to bother the security personnel in the least.

A security guard was in charge of a leather bound ledger where each person recorded their name, time of arrival, date, signature and so on.

"Please don't forget to fill in the time of departure when you leave!"

He was not having a good day. An elegant lady in a colourful sari had just lost her temper and was now screaming at him.

"I want to speak to the manager!"

While the heartfelt complaint might have had an effect in an exclusive five star hotel, I thought it wouldn't work too well in an embassy. She never got a chance to meet and speak to a manager. The security guard, assisted by military personnel, told her to calm down, threatening to escort her back out to Knightsbridge.

"How rude!" she said, before storming out of her own accord, shouting further abuse.

After a scramble to fill in all register entries with the official pen tied on a short string, I was told to take a lift to the third floor. I walked along a corridor of small offices opening along both sides. Everyone seemed extremely busy. With no signs to help me, I walked into an office asking where I should go to have my interview.

"Do you have an appointment?"

"No. I called yesterday and was told to just come along..."

"Ok. Just take a seat."

Unless I walked to a desk and asked someone to leave, there weren't any chairs to be seen.

Noticing I was still standing, they eventually pointed to another office further along. This was the right place and hidden behind a door was a comfortable black leather sofa. The switchboard lady sitting by a desk on the side, patiently answered a never ending barrage of phone calls. The only relief to her frustration was to sometimes question the caller's sanity by raising her eyebrows or, in extreme cases, to let her body slouch back on the chair while staring at the ceiling. If I thought I would be grilled with difficult questions prying into all my fake hotel bookings and invitation letters I was left disappointed.

A smartly dressed officer introduced himself and sat next to me. He asked to see the documents that I had already submitted.

"A LOI letter!" he said surprised. "That is what I needed."

"Yes... I sent you this already last week."

"I didn't get it." he said.

I was sure that after paying so much money for it I must have sent it. I felt frustrated. A day wasted to come all the way to London for something I had already done. I could have thrown a tantrum like the elegant lady but I knew it wouldn't help me. I kept my composure, helped by a perfectly timed example of kindness. An elderly man walked in with a large tray full of fresh halwa sweets. Surely I won't be offered any, I thought, still grumpy. He proceeded to offer them to all the staff around me until my turn arrived.

"Freshly made pakistani sweets?"

Embassies, no matter where, are notorious for unhelpful and miserable experiences. Waiting rooms are filled with people whose moods are just as low as those waiting for an appointment at the dentist. Despite the hiccups I was quite impressed.

The High Commission had redeemed itself, they tasted delicious.

"Don't worry." I was reassured.

"You have plenty of time and you will get your Visa."

All I had to do now was to fill in my time of departure on the register and escape. There was a clash between those walking in and those walking out, accompanied by the noise of the jammed and flashing metal detector. Nobody really knew whose turn it was to get hold of the pen. I began by patiently waiting but I was getting nowhere. I had to be assertive and fight. In the end, unable to take hold of the ledger, I asked for some help. The security guard, by now quite hysterical, waved his hand, telling me I could go.

"But the departure time...?" I asked.

"I will fill that in", he said, "don't worry."

After a month of trying, I was finally issued the coveted permit. I was really about to visit Pakistan.

Walking towards the gate for my Dubai to Islamabad flight I started feeling a little out of place. My colourful clothes were in strident contrast to an increasingly uniform crowd of blacks and whites. My clean shave was also not popular; most were sporting long wiry beards that would have taken me years of patient waiting. I sat down and simmered in the awareness that I stood out like a sore thumb. I boarded the plane and met Shamiz, my next seat neighbour. Before I had had a chance to sit down, he extended his arm for a handshake. Like many of his countrymen, he was a Dubai expatriate working hard for a few years to bring back home some savings. After a brief introduction and some chit chat, he scribbled down his mobile phone number on a piece of paper, telling me to call him should I need anything.

"My uncle is meeting me at the airport and will drive me home."

"Please come with us!" he said. "I would love to show you around my hometown for a few days and have you as my guest."

I struggled to find some polite words to decline his kind offer.
He was from Peshawar, not far from the border with Afghanistan and well out of my planned way.

Once we had arrived at the new Benazir Bhutto International Airport, we walked together towards the luggage belts. Delivered by the most gentle female voice, a repetitive message was broadcast through the terminal Public Announcements system.

"We would like to remind passengers that drug trafficking is against the law. Passengers contravening the law will be punished with a death sentence."

I wasn't carrying any, but hearing those final two words made me feel rather nervous. On the alert, I moved my backpack to the front, suspiciously scanning everything and everyone that was moving nearby.

A three hours car journey in the middle of the night awaited Shamiz and his family. Despite this, after greeting his relatives at the arrival lobby, he asked them to wait. He helped me search for a money exchange, walking with me all the way until we found it. Only then did he wish me a good holiday and waived his farewell.

For the first time I felt on my own. This wasn't going to last that long. The next challenge was finding a taxi to drive me to the hotel I had reserved. Taxi drivers walked towards me eager to assist. Ismail offered some help next. He was Saudi born but had been studying at Islamabad University for the last three years. With impeccable English combined with local skills, he haggled down the price and invited me to share a taxi with him. He felt ashamed by the taxi driver's attempt to rip me off.

Once we reached my hotel he insisted on following me, checking my room to ensure I was getting a decent deal. Not happy with the loud noise coming from the air conditioning he negotiated a discounted rate. I unloaded my luggage and, despite my insistence, he refused to take any payment for my share of the journey.

"You are in my country." he said "You are my guest."

I later found this to be a common refrain. Had such care been offered by a close relative I would have felt very pleased but this was coming from a total stranger. Before we parted he handed me another phone number I could call should I ever need to.

Islamabad is not exactly Paris. I hadn't come all the way to visit Pakistan Monument or the contemporary Faisal Mosque. I had come to see some mighty mountains, and Islamabad was at the end of the plains and the perfect gateway. Despite feeling tired and jet-lagged, after a night's rest, I decided to start cycling. I was eager to move away from the hooting symphony of the city traffic and its pollution. The beginning of my itinerary had been a little ill planned. The road was uphill for most of the day and distances way too long to start with. Half way through, I felt tired and beaten by the scorching heat of the midday sun. In a corner by the side of a steep switchback I passed by a tiny concrete kiosk with panoramic view of the hills around. It had cement benches along the sides and, most tempting of all, the chance to sit a little in the shade. Not able to read any Urdu, I couldn't exactly tell what it really was. It could have been a bus stop, a birdwatching spot, a toilet with a view or maybe a combination of all these and anything in between. I lay down exhausted. Staring at the ceiling, I began reading the chalk and graffiti scribbles. For some reason they were mostly written in the Roman alphabet and in English. Walls were filled with the love for Aisha. Having regained my strength, I was about to leave when an old man selling roasted corn on the cob asked me if I wanted some. In that heat it was not appealing. He then asked if I wanted something strong to smoke instead.

"No thanks."

It was the last thing my lungs needed. I would have collapsed back on that hard bench even if a tad happier. There were no foreigners to be seen up these mountains. I was the centre of attention, gaining instant celebrity status. Motor-bikers kept coasting next to me asking lots of questions. Drivers shouted and cheered me on; that demanded some sort of appreciative reply, or at least a smile. A couple of times I stopped at little shops to stock up on water and energy snacks. They didn't let me pay for anything. After a brief chat, someone would usually invite me to stay at their house for the night.

"You are in Pakistan. You are our guest." they all said.

- Kholian, PAKISTAN -

I was humbled by the generosity of people who were often much poorer, materially, than me. I just about made it to Murree, the mountain resort where Islamabad folk head to breathe some fresh air and escape briefly from the summer heat.

There were always plenty of fans on the road to cheer me on; the start of the tour had definitely been a success. For the first few days I tried to respond to their enthusiasm, but I felt exhausted trying to match all that goodwill. Kind and well meaning as they were, they crossed my path only briefly and once in a lifetime. As for myself, I was stuck in an endless chain of chance encounters. Of course I was pleased, but it also meant waving my arms to the verge of cramps and telling them I came from Italy a hundred times. I bored myself declaring my love of Pakistan and its people and announcing I was on my way to the border with China. They glanced at my unusual bicycle and I could tell from their faces that they didn't quite believe me. I had to be a little more careful and conserve some of my energies for the cycling or I would end up risking a greetings burnout.

Pakistanis were keen on pictures and video reporting. When they couldn't catch me on one of my breaks off the bike, drivers would slow down and coast by my side. Pulling down their car windows, they asked me if I wouldn't mind stopping for a selfie. Often requests for a short picture turned into lengthy live video interviews. The improvised reporter would ask me where I came from and what I thought of their country. I developed a well rehearsed drill with convincing answers. Whatever was said they loved to hear a foreigner telling them how impressed I was by their unique hospitality. A couple of times these requests turned into commercials.

"By the way I work for an outdoor gear company in Karachi."

"Would you mind saying a few good words about our products?"

Not to sound rude, I complied with that too, praising the qualities of clothes I had never seen let alone worn.

I reached the border of Punjab, passing under a large blue border sign.

'Welcome to Khyber Pakhtunkhwa.' it said, 'Land of hospitality.'

The ability of Pakistanis to make a traveller welcome was way beyond anything I had ever experienced. Thinking about it, this was consistent in all the Muslim countries I had visited. Guests enjoy a special place in Islam and offering hospitality is very much a part of their faith. As a bicycle traveller along their roads, I was in the lucky position of being everybody's guest. Act of kindness were so common that I felt embarrassed by them. During one of my 'the road is too steep' walks, a little truck stopped and waited for me. A smiling driver asked if I needed a ride. As I always do on such occasions, I thanked him but resisted all temptations. I am never in a rush and as much as possible I want to cycle or walk these roads all the way. In Khaira Gali I stopped for breakfast at a roadside café and met Nadir and his family from Multan in Punjab. After a quick handshake and introduction he ran to his car and returned with two large mangoes and a packet of crisps for me.

"Mangoes from Multan of course." he said proudly.

I later discovered these were famous all over the country as some of the best. He sat down and talked with me, telling me about his family's journey to these mountains. I then briefly lost sight of him. He returned, waving goodbye.

"By the way...your bill has been taken care of."

I tried to stand my ground and refuse, but he wouldn't take my money no matter how hard I tried.

"Mashallah. Enjoy Pakistan!"

Mashallah. I quickly learnt the different translations of that word that I heard so often.

'May God protect you' or 'what God wanted has happened'. I liked the way it sounded and liked both meanings.

I crossed more foggy mountains before diving down to the hustle and bustle of Abbottabad, briefly joining part of the Karakoram Highway. This city had acquired unwelcome notoriety when the world discovered that it was where Osama Bin Laden had lived during his last few years in hiding. Along a busy road I heard some shouting. I thought it must be yet another request for a selfie. Tired after a long day of cycling I decided to turn a deaf ear and ignore it. A minute later a van was slowing down at my side, a boy holding one of my spare tyres. It had obviously come loose and dropped out on the road somewhere.

I desperately needed an HBL Bank ATM machine to withdraw more cash. I had tried other banks, but they had consistently thrown out fingerprint-scan requests, and 'server is down' messages before spitting out my card. Credit cards were never accepted, only cash so far, wherever I had been. I waited for an elderly man with bandy legs and a wispy beard to complete his transaction. He came out shivering in the traditional light cotton dress called Shalwar Kameez. It was my turn to enter the tiny ATM boot. The air conditioning had been turned on full blast, mimicking conditions of a severe Siberian winter. Habib Bank once more produced the goods. As I walked back outside, moving in an instant from subzero temperatures to plus thirty, I noticed the same man was waiting for me. I had already complete trust in Pakistanis' honesty. Anywhere else I would have been concerned, wondering if I was about to be robbed. The gentleman shook my hand, introducing himself with family name, title and profession, and said:

"Is everything ok?" "Is there anything I can do for you?"

I laughed and told him that unless he could cycle for me all the way to Balakot, I was fine.

"Welcome to Pakistan sir".

This is the kind of attention to detail and service that you get if you can afford a luxury suite at a Ritz Carlton hotel. It is rarely bestowed on you for free by total strangers.

It took one year from my life span to get out of Abbottabad. For an hour I subjected my lungs to the inhalation of dark diesel fumes spouting out of 1950's engines. As I reached the limit of the city I spotted on the top of a hill a familiar Mc Donald sign. I am not a fan of fast food chains but seeing one here I was intrigued. I reached the gate, where a security guard was a little puzzled to see a poor westerner on a bicycle. He nevertheless raised the bar and allowed me into an almost empty car park. Outside the main entrance I was asked to go through a scanner not unlike the one at the High Commission in Knightsbridge. What was different here were the two guards with dangling Kalashnikov rifles. My bag full of gadgets had set off the system's alarm. A bag search was necessary. I guess one never knows, but I would have made for an unlikely bomber cyclist. Finally, I was allowed in. The large place had a total of twenty staff eager to serve a handful of customers. They were scrambling for work, fighting to clean already spotless windows. A customer visiting seemed quite an event. There was a general dash to the cashier to take my order.

"Thank you sir. Please sit down. The double mac, chips and Pepsi will be served at your table."

Between security checks and biting a burger, about twenty minutes had passed. It was officially the slowest food I had ordered in Pakistan. Any street vendor could produce a full meal and freshly baked bread in a matter of minutes. It was expensive too. Maybe the long wait was part of the experience, a way to justify the high prices and to make it special.

At Mansehra, after days roaming wild and free I was stopped at a police check post for the first time. This was a common thing that I had read about in the accounts of other cyclists. The government, while pushing to bring back tourism, was also going to extreme lengths to ensure safety. Independent cyclists, like mountaineers, freaked them out as they couldn't easily be controlled. It was not uncommon for a police escort to be despatched on a mission to follow us. I had read how sometimes they insisted on travellers being driven to the safe hands of the next control post. Tariq, the officer on duty, politely asked me to take a seat and began to fill in all my details. With long Visa numbers and cumbersome foreign addresses to deal with, it was a slow process.

"Don't you have strips of paper with all the details already filled in?" he asked.

"That's what a couple of German cyclists gave me last month, it was really quick..."

I have always had great respect for German planning and efficiency. However, coming from Italy, I had a good excuse.

He completed all his registry entries before asking where I would spend the night.

"I am not sure. I hope to reach Balakot and will see how that goes..."

He then asked for a planned route of my next few days.

"Please wait five minutes," he said "I need to let my boss know."

"What do you think about Pakistan? Is it safe?" he asked.

It was a weird question coming from a policeman. I thought he should know.

I didn't fancy a ride in a jeep. I had to show some confidence, even though I had barely survived a Russian roulette round cycling through an atrocious traffic jam in Qalandarabad.

"Wonderful! Very safe! Everyone is so friendly!" I said.

He was pleased to hear my reassurances. Phone calls were made until Tariq said I was free to go. He handed me a brochure listing police telephone numbers for all districts in Khyber Pakhtunkhwa.

"You never know." he said. He still had some doubts.

As far as traffic was concerned I had survived the worst. I was now heading up for more fresh mountain air. After climbing the first few hills, a landscape of rising peaks and green pastures appeared in the distance. I cycled most of the afternoon surrounded by bushes of cannabis plants in flower. There was so much of it that it was safe to assume it must have been legal, at least for medical purposes... At the end of a long, straight stretch I noticed a motorcyclist sitting on his bike by the side of the road, waiting. I stopped and started chatting with him.

"Italian? One month visa?" he suddenly said.

"Welcome. I am undercover police."

After my newly acquired celebrity status, my ego was now boosted by full VIP attention. A private escort all to myself! What a treat, I couldn't believe it. He then disappeared, never to be seen again.

I stopped to eat at a restaurant and in order to avoid another free meal I thought it would be wise to pay my bill beforehand. Locals joined me in the garden outside. I met a lawyer and his family visiting from Karachi. He was intrigued by my stamina.

"You must be brave or completely mad!" he said.

"We Pakistanis wouldn't dream of cycling on our own up these mountains..."

"Have a safe journey...by the way your bill has been taken care of."

"No. It's impossible." I said with a grin.
"I have already paid for it."

"I know. They will return your money. You are in Pakistan so you are our guest."

Even paying in advance didn't work!

I was following the Kaghan valley all the way up the 4173 metres of Babusar mountain. On the western edge of the Himalayan range, vertical green slopes rose on either side. I had my first striking views, teasers of what would follow later along the Karakoram Highway. I reached Kiwai, a little hamlet built on a busy, sharp bend. Here a mountain stream had been tamed and turned into a refreshing open air dining room. A tarpaulin roof had been stretched across, resting on poles fixed by the banks on the sides. Plastic chairs and tables had been arranged half-submerged in fresh flowing waters. Customers could sit in the shade and enjoy their meals while cooling their feet at the same time. This creative use of nature proved a success. The place was buzzing with tourists and families. Six kids attracted by a foreigner came and sat right in front of me, eager to practise some English. I told them I was Italian at which point they got even more excited.

Their dad lived in Italy. They started calling him and the rest of the family. A few elderly women joined us at the table, then the wife, sister-in-law and a few more relatives before the man himself who spoke fluent Italian. A headcount was necessary to ensure everyone was there. They were twenty two.

I continued my ascent, interrupted here and there by selfie requests. A young man in a Manchester United red shirt begged me to stop.

"Please stop" he said, asking if he could take a photograph of us together.

"It's the first time I have ever seen a foreigner around here."

I felt like the last standing Panda in a city zoo.

That they weren't seeing many foreigners around here was clear. Later a couple asked whether I was Chinese.

I went for a late lunch in a village restaurant and chatted with four young men sitting beside me. Having finished my meal, I knew I had to face the usual fight in order to pay. As always I lost.

"Why is everybody paying for my meals around here?" I asked them.

"This is our custom with guests" one of them said, and continued:

"Westerners think Pakistanis are all terrorists."

"Once you return to your country please tell your friends that we are peaceful and generous people."

"Maybe one day they will also come and find out for themselves."

I imagined a Pakistan with mass tourism and people facing bankruptcy as a result of paying tourists' bills. I was adjusting nicely to all this care and attention. I worried how I would cope once the holiday was over. I imagined myself dealing with the sudden loss of popularity, forced to pay all my invoices and thoroughly depressed.

There were four police posts along the way. Only once did they request that I stop. Information about my imminent arrival had been relayed and they knew all about me. I showed them my passport and after a brief chat it was time for a series of selfies, this time with guns. Later that day I was twice offered a lift, I was given three apples and several more people stopped their cars simply to talk to me. One of them felt sorry for not having anything he could give me.

He apologised before asking "Please tell me what I can do for you?"

It was hard to get a decent night's sleep. There were no cockerels around here, unlike in Thailand. However, every morning, no matter where, I was woken up by Fajr, the early morning prayer. This started at a precise moment, scientifically determined by complicated astrophysical formulae. Vaguely before sunrise, whatever the time, it was always too early. Perky Imams interrupted the peace and silence and started passionately chanting verses, each in his own individual style and tone, waking me up with a jolt. The Kaghan mosque had a top notch amplifying system. An array of loudspeakers projected sound in all directions, enhanced by some kind of reverb. The voice echoed, bouncing around the mountains and giving the impression that prayers were indeed coming down to us from the sky. The Imam was obviously pleased and delivered himself with gusto, showing off an outstanding vocal range.

I had a long chat with the hotel owner and discovered that the 2005 Kashmir earthquake, one of the strongest ever recorded, had deeply affected these valleys.

Buildings and bridges around Balakot had pretty much been flattened. There had been a big international rescue plan that he still talked about fondly. Shahzim lived in his recently built hotel during the tourist season and then spent the rest of the year in Abbottabad. He was friendly enough to satisfy my morbid curiosity about Osama Bin Laden.

"Did people know he lived there?" I dared to ask.

He was adamant nobody did.

"If anyone at all knew," he said "it was the secret services."

I wasn't surprised by his answer. Some of those same policemen in disguise had stopped me and called me by name. It happened that day and it made me feel at home. At one such stop in a beautiful but desolate location, an army guy was so bored with his own company that he asked if I could stay a little longer and have lunch with him. I had a feeling he was desperately lonely but I had to move on. I shook hands and chatted with many people. They were all most generous to me. Between Naran and Jalkhand I received three chocolate bars, dried apricots, two packets of biscuits, a mango and a boiled egg.

The Naran river descended slowly, surrounded by towering mountains. Pakistanis love perfume. Every now and then a packed bus would overtake me leaving a sweet trail of scent lingering in the air. I reached an altitude of three thousand metres; it was getting dark and I felt a little tired. A grey van with blacked-out windows coming down the other way stopped in front of me. The driver signalled me to stop. I shook my head and told him I had to go.

"No. Please stop!" he insisted.

As he said this, a man came running out from the van. I immediately recognized the familiar face of Salman Mushtaq. We had never met in person but I had seen him in pictures and he looked very familiar. We laughed and hugged, thinking what a funny place the world is. Salman was many things. Owner of a travel agent in Faisalabad, tourist guide, mountaineer, motorbiker and an excellent photographer. Some of his landscape pictures had appeared on my computer screen many months before. I had got in touch with him and exchanged a few emails in which he shared information about Pakistan. He was aware that I would be cycling over these mountains around this time and had kept an eye out for me. He had just completed a tour and was taking his clients back to the city. He grabbed a bag of snacks and sweets and gave it to me, saying he would come back with a group of Malaysian motorbikers the following week.

At long last, after days of cycling, I reached the top of Babusar.

- Babusar Pass, PAKISTAN -

I was not breaking any speed records. A slow progress with a detour to Murree had taken me from the plains to a height of over four thousand metres. I moved through unspoilt valleys with a handful of villages. Views were impressive, only tempered by the abject poverty I could see by the sides of the road. Scattered here and there were hamlets of mud dwellings and battered tents. Colorless and torn, they were still bearing the faded logos of aid organisations that had helped in the aftermath of the earthquake. The lucky ones were the shepherds with their herds of goats. Others farmed the arid land, struggling to grow whatever they could to try and get by. Then there were the children. Often walking and playing on these roads, they took advantage of the occasional traffic to beg for a few rupees or some food.

They were the first to spot my bike from a distance, and always got very excited. I could hear them shouting and calling each other. Whether it was Urdu or a local dialect, I could only understand one word that sounded like English.

"Cycle, Cycle!" I would hear them scream.

They weren't sure what to make of me and rarely asked me for anything. Given how slow I was, they most enjoyed following me, staring at me and my bicycle with their beautiful green eyes and their dusty faces. One boy followed me uphill, for what must have been a good ten minutes, walking fast by my side. I heard the unusual sound of some western music playing. I turned towards him and met his gaze. He was keen to show me his most precious possession, an ancient mobile phone he was probably given.

Few people I met asked if I was Muslim. When I told them I wasn't, they never looked disappointed and treated me exactly the same. It was Sunday, and hordes of Pakistani tourists had escaped the cities, driving many hours to breathe the fresh air and spot a few patches of snow.

Having reached the top of the pass I was mobbed for more pictures. An elderly policeman, as proud of himself as if he had been put in charge of the entire mountain, came to help. I asked him whether there was an official stone with the name and the height of the pass.

"Of course there is. Please follow me!"

He escorted me through the crowd, telling them to part to let me and Bronte stand right in front of the brick wall by the stone signpost:

'Babusar Top (13700 ft)'

I was seeking adventure and was about to find it. I began my descent down the steep road moving from Khyber Pakhtunkhwa into Gilgit Baltistan. The light was gently fading now and I planned to stay at Babusar village about halfway down the other side. The policeman I had just met said he would follow me, coming down by car with a friend. As I reached the village hotel he was waiting for me. He asked me to sit on a wooden bench and offered me some tea. Also waiting was a crowd of locals who surrounded me. They stared at me as if I had just landed from Mars. I couldn't blame them at all as it had taken me a week to spot my first foreigners, a couple of Germans who were cycling the opposite way. The crowd was a little overpowering but so far I had met only good-natured people and had no reason to doubt these weren't the same. A dark room with a mattress on the floor was shown to me. It was very basic, but given it was almost 6pm and the light was fading, I thought I would take it. What happened next confused me. A younger policeman arrived and started arguing with the one I had met earlier. Nobody spoke much English but it was soon obvious that he was not happy for me to stay there.

"Safety issue." he said looking at me.

They were the only few words I could understand.

He gestured I should descend to the town of Chilas, thirty kilometres further downhill.

The elderly policeman was more reassuring, but for some reason I started to feel a little uncomfortable and decided to do the most stupid thing, which could have cost me dearly. I lost all good sense and decided to start cycling downhill. Not finding accommodation on my previous trips had never been a big issue as I carried a tent with me. I would find a quiet spot before nightfall and that was that. This time was different. For the first time I felt a little uneasy and still heard those two words ringing in my ears. By the time I had barely covered half the distance it got too dark. I started thinking I should pitch my tent somewhere but then gave up. Safety issue...

I stopped two motorcyclists descending the mountain and asked them if they were going to Chilas. They took care of me as best they could. One stayed in front of me and the other behind so that their lights could help me guess where I was going. They often checked whether I was near enough, slowing down if I wasn't. I tried my best to follow the line of the one in front of me. Half of me thought this was just crazy while the other half felt the adrenaline rush and was convinced I would get away with it. At a certain point the inevitable happened. I moved a little too far behind and, not able to see where I was going, found myself falling off with a clumsy somersault.

In the end I hadn't got away with it. Able to get back on my feet I checked the bike, thinking it must be a complete wreck. I was amazed to realise that it all seemed in good order instead. My leg was aching but I was able to cycle on. Having reached the junction with the Karakoram Highway, I spotted a police check post. Finally I could ask for some help. I couldn't thank my two saviours as they sped on and disappeared fast into the night. A policeman walked me across the road into their little station and invited me to spend the night there. He offered me some of his food, but I had gone through too much to feel hungry. I was somehow relieved to have reached safety.

Bones seemed to be intact, although I was limping badly. I sat chatting with three policemen before they offered me a shower. They all agreed that I had been given some bad advice up in Babusar. By now I couldn't agree more with them. In hindsight, even if there had been a genuine safety issue, the chances of something bad happening to me were negligible compared to the risks of such a kamikaze night descent. I cursed myself for doing something so incredibly stupid. Were I to do it again, I am sure the same thing would happen. It was sticky and hot inside the little police station. Four metal beds were moved outside and placed next to each other on the lawn by the roadside.

Things learnt today:

it is dumb to cycle at night when you cannot see where you are going...

I couldn't sleep much due to the pain in my leg and the noise of the traffic. Until midnight the station radio barked out emergency calls in Urdu. At least I could look up and admire a glorious black sky full of stars. I woke up on the bed in the garden early in the morning. Three policemen were unfolding their carpets towards Mecca, before starting their shift. Zain, whom I had met the previous night, was the least endearing of them. Unlike pretty much all the Pakistanis I had encountered so far, he was not someone who could easily smile.

"You should get up and pray!" he said firmly, looking at me still lying in bed.

I needed all the help I could get, it was not a good time to argue with him. As I tried to get up my right leg wouldn't let me. I wondered whether something was indeed broken, filling my mind with worries. A young policeman, who was heating up some chai, realised I was in pain and hand-signed if I wanted to smoke something. I was in a police station but it didn't surprise me. Rewinding what had happened the previous night only upset me further.

I thought the trip was well over. Hopping about on one leg, I told Zain I needed to visit a hospital; I needed to get some crutches.

"This is a poor town, they won't have crutches." he said.

That didn't reassure me. If the trip was over I had to be able to return to Islamabad and walk onto a plane.

Hafeez was the first policeman I met when I rolled down the mountain in tatters. He had a completely different nature and was more than willing to help.

"We will take you to the hospital this morning and help you to get back, don't worry."

I wobbled inside the station, where I had dumped all my belongings, and began planning what to do next. It dawned on me that even if I was to get some crutches, I couldn't take everything with me. I could possibly carry my rucksack on my shoulders, but bike, tent, tools and other unnecessary weights would have to be left behind. I couldn't believe that after seven years of epic adventures this was where I would have to abandon Bronte. I know it sounds sentimental; it was only a bicycle - but it had carried me around the world and never let me down, even when my recklessness had crashed it.
Zain sat down in front of me, assessing my misery. He didn't really help.

"You leave the bike to me." he said.

I was fuming, but I knew he was right, what was the choice?

I stuffed as much as I could into my backpack, and left the assembled bicycle and all the rest on the other side.

They drove me to the local hospital. Chilas didn't look a happy place. It was dry, hot and dusty, and even among Pakistanis it had a reputation for not being friendly. I had read about it before the trip. It probably didn't deserve it, but the town had never recovered from a series of brutal murders that had happened five years earlier. A dozen western mountaineers were shot dead at Nanga Parbat base camp by a group of extremists. Most of them were from Chilas and other villages in the area. Possibly this also contributed to my poor decision to keep riding into the night and to believe the warnings of one policeman. I moved through the gloomy corridors of a messy looking building, supported by Hafeez and Zain. There weren't any other patients waiting. The first doctor checked my leg and the bruising and gave me a glimmer of hope by saying there might be nothing broken. After two injections, the x-ray confirmed it.

I felt greatly relieved. He confirmed it was muscular pain resulting from the fall; and the news got even better. After two injections and prescribing some painkillers, he told me I should be able to continue my journey and ride on further. Given the pain I had felt early in the morning I couldn't believe it, but those were the only words I wanted to hear. I was driven back to the police station, where I started to reassemble my gear, euphoric I could go on. Whatever injections I had been given, they were working.

"Well what can I say..." said Zain.

"I am sad that I won't be riding your bike but happy that you can continue."

He still hadn't shown a single smile in two days but he had redeemed himself a little and, by following Hafeez's example, had helped me out. Within the span of an hour, the fate of the journey had flipped itself upside down and changed completely.

- Rakaposhi, PAKISTAN -

I was back on the bike, finally riding on the mythical Karakoram Highway, along the Indus river. The stark landscape was a great contrast after a week of green valleys. A desert strip of rocks and sand was framed by the giant Karakoram mountains. It was sweltering hot, but I didn't mind in the least and made it all the way to Raikot Bridge. Scores of tourists were coming down from Fairy Meadows where Nanga Parbat can be seen in all its splendour. I had been planning to do the short trek myself the following day but I knew my leg wouldn't let me. It was much easier to cycle than walk and by evening it was once again hurting. I felt frustrated, but considered myself lucky to at least be able to see its majestic shape from a distance.

I reached Gilgit but was still limping. Following the suggestion of the hotel manager I headed to the military hospital. He said it was the best place in the whole region to have a proper check-up. Military compounds in Pakistan were way ahead of the rest of the country. A taxi driver took me there, waited for me to complete all the tests and helped with translating. I moved back and forth between different buildings before being asked to wait for the Chief Medical officer's verdict. A youngish chap with a 'God almighty' complex walked into the waiting room wearing an elegant silk blue garment and shining leather shoes. All the military personnel and nurses stood straight and still, giving him a military salute. I was invited into his office and he told me that all was good.

"Muscular inflammation." he said.

He seemed sure of himself, although I could hardly walk. A few more medicines were supplied by a pharmacist, who also offered me and the taxi driver a refreshing pink drink. After at least one hour spent with me, he drove me back to the hotel. Having arrived, he refused to take any more money than the regular fare we had agreed. I forced twice the amount into his hand and he took it reluctantly. He deserved much more and it was not much to me. Anywhere else in the world a taxi driver would have shown at least some impatience and put me on a waiting meter.

I was told to take a break for a couple of days before riding on to the Hunza Valley, which was to be the highlight of the trip. It was a special day in Gilgit. Shia Muslims were celebrating Ashura, the holiest day of the year. For reasons of safety, the city had been put in complete 'shut-down' mode. The shops' metal grids were lowered and the telephone lines and internet had been temporarily stopped. Pakistan felt safe to me, but these celebrations in the past had ended in trouble. It was a good day to stay put and nurse my leg pain.

After three days of rest in a hotel room I couldn't put up with any more waiting. I hadn't recovered that much, but cycling was more bearable than walking. I was crawling along, but the scenery before my eyes was best appreciated in slow motion. This narrow strip of tarmac twisted and turned around bare ochre mountains. I could admire peaks over six thousand metres all around me. I had left the Indus far behind me and was now following the Hunza river. Nothing else had changed, people still smiled and waved at me. Despite the unnecessary warnings, I had never felt as safe as here, cycling in a country I had always been told was too dangerous. Even Pakistani stray dogs were tame and never chased me.

When I told people my name was Gianni, they started smiling. The pronunciation sounded pretty close to moon in Urdu and they liked it. I still seemed Chinese to a lot of them and they greeted me accordingly. 'Ni hao' I would often hear. We were a short drive away from the border with China and the two governments, involved in many large joint projects, were also close. Chinese money and expertise was pouring in, building roads, dams and tunnels. I loved the Pakistani invention of putting sleeping areas inside restaurants. When I had finished my meal I could always find some raised platforms with mattresses and pillows and join the truck drivers for a nap. There were lots of motorbikes on the road, sometimes carrying families of four. I was in awe when I spotted women sitting sidesaddles behind their husbands. Their long dresses probably demanded it, but it seemed such a risky way to travel. I wondered how they could do this daily and get to live long lives.

I spent the night in the mountain village of Jaffar Abbad, where the locals welcomed me with curiosity and interest. The guest house owner showed me a basic room, charging me five dollars. Upon my request he provided me with a complimentary bucket of hot water to rinse away my sweat. Opposite my room was a newly opened burger place. A little tired, and fed up with lentils, flat bread and fried eggs, I craved some comfort food. I remembered how bad meat in the mountains of Thailand had put me on a toilet seat for three entire days. I asked the guy if I could have a look at it. He opened the fridge and showed me a tray of beef burgers whose colour didn't convince me. With the frequent power cuts I had witnessed, I was sure they couldn't be that fresh. However, for some reason I still ordered one with chips and a drink. I sat in the garden, waiting and regretting my choice. Only one thing was worse than limping on holiday: limping with bouts of diarrhoea. Once the burger had been served I knew what had to be done. Timing a good throw when the chef wasn't looking, I flipped the burger like a frisbee, as far as I could. At least I ate the bun and the fries, which were not that bad.

Many villagers were hanging around and I had the chance to talk to quite a few of them. It was a Friday, and in the evening everyone disappeared to the mosque for prayers. For two hours the Mullah delivered a long sermon through distorted loudspeakers. At times his voice sounded kind and gentle, then suddenly he would burst into loud rants that rattled the valley. I shut my door with the bolt and locked it just in case. When it was all over I cheered. Peace and quiet were restored. I entered the Lower Hunza Valley and cycled through the landscapes that had motivated me to come here. After spotting Nanga Parbat in the distance it was time to get closer to Rakaposhi, also known as Dunami in the local language, 'mother of myst'. At almost eight thousand meters, it was the 26th highest peak in the world, but what was most unique about it was the fact that it rose straight up from the road. I sat down at the popular viewpoint sipping sweet Chai while staring at its beautiful shapes wrapped in ice and thick snow: six thousand metres of uninterrupted slope that, I later read, was the highest on Earth.

While the morning threatened rain, by the late afternoon it had changed. Mountain peaks played hide and seek with clouds and mist. In a couple of days I reached Attabad lake. Ten years before a chunk of mountain had collapsed, blocking the river flow. A freak event of nature, where lives were lost, had created a turquoise lake where tourists were now rowing boats. It's cyan colour reminded me of Lake Louise and all the other lakes along the Icefield Parkway. I reached the entrance of a series of tunnels. The longest of them was four kilometres long with no lights inside.

- Passu Cones, PAKISTAN -

After what I had gone through, I felt I could not take any more risks. I sat by the side of the road waiting for a ride. A couple of employees from the National Highway Authority turned up with a pickup car and offered to take me to the other side. It started spitting some rain and a gusty wind started blowing. I took cover for the time being in a little shop, chatting with the owner while eating some cake. He was a Tajik like many people around this border area. Their native language was Wakhi. I had never heard of it but this dialect was spoken in parts of China, Russia, Afghanistan and Pakistan. For the first time, someone wasn't too keen on the Chinese. He frequently crossed the border to import shoes and clothes that he would sell in the markets of Gilgit.

"Our governments are close but I don't really like them…" he said.

"Few people there are friendly and nobody is free."

"By now they must know me, yet each time I cross the border they search me from head to toe."

After more twisting and turning, I got my first clear views of the Cathedral. This journey ended where it had all started, with Salman's picture of the Passu Cones. It was a unique feeling to be rolling down that same straight road whose beauty had stunned me months earlier back home. With one and a half legs and having taken my last painkiller, I had to accept that I couldn't possibly make it up the Khunjerab pass. The Chinese border was a couple of days away but it would have been too much of a strain. Such an eventful journey, that had almost turned into a failure, couldn't have ended in a better way.

I had planned this to be Bronte's final trip. After many flights and thousands of miles of cycling over the last seven years, the only thing that had been missing was a tumble. Even that was now achieved. Since the day I had unwrapped this new, fragile looking bicycle, I had been wondering when it would eventually fail. In the end that never happened. Bronte was still going strong; it was the cyclist first who had almost been broken.

Pakistan Zindabad!

Printed in Great Britain
by Amazon

37885729R00131